Mary
THE MOTHER OF JESUS

CAMILLE FRONK OLSON

DESERET BOOK

Salt Lake City, Utah

© 2012 Camille Fronk Olson

All rights reserved. No part of this book may be reproduced in any form or by any means without permission in writing from the publisher, Deseret Book Company, P. O. Box 30178, Salt Lake City, Utah 84130. This work is not an official publication of The Church of Jesus Christ of Latter-day Saints. The views expressed herein are the responsibility of the author and do not necessarily represent the position of the Church or of Deseret Book Company.

DESERET BOOK is a registered trademark of Deseret Book Company.

Visit us at DeseretBook.com

Library of Congress Cataloging-in-Publication Data
Olson, Camille Fronk, author.
  Mary, the mother of Jesus / Camille Fronk Olson.
      pages cm.
  Includes bibliographical references.
  ISBN 978-1-60907-005-2 (hardbound : alk. paper)
1. Mary, Blessed Virgin, Saint—Biography. 2. Mormon Church—Doctrines. I. Title.
  BX8643.M37O47 2012
  232.91—dc23   2012003563

Printed in the United States of America
Publishers Printing, Salt Lake City, UT

10 9 8 7 6 5 4 3 2 1

Contents

1. Mary, the Mother of Jesus 1
2. Prophecies concerning Mary 7
3. Childhood of Jewish Girls 11
4. Jewish Marriage Customs 17
5. The Annunciation in Nazareth 21
6. Joseph 29
7. Mary's Lineage 33
8. Mary's Visit to Elisabeth 41
9. Jesus' Birth in Bethlehem 51

CONTENTS

10. The Law of Moses and Childbirth 61

11. The Escape to Egypt 69

12. Mothering the Child Jesus 77

13. During the Savior's Mortal Ministry 87

14. Jesus' Suffering and Death 99

15. After the Resurrection 105

Notes 109

Illustration Credits 115

to

ROBERTA OF TREMONTON

my mother

My soul doth magnify the Lord, and my spirit hath rejoiced in God my Saviour

LUKE 1:46–47

CHAPTER ONE

Mary, the Mother of Jesus

Fewer than ten days in the life of Mary, the mother of Jesus, are revealed in scripture, but all generations since her lifetime have been taught about her and have called her blessed. She was the mother of the Son of God—a loving mother during very challenging times. And she was an exemplary disciple of Jesus Christ, an inspired witness of God's gracious favor, and a guardian of remarkable truths. Unique among women in all of scripture, Mary is never portrayed in a negative light but is universally reverenced. Every mention of her signals purity, goodness, and discipleship.

The actual meaning of the Hebrew form of *Mary* is uncertain, but the suggestion of "excellence" implied in a related Hebrew word meaning "height, exalted, or to give strength to" seems appropriate for the mother of the Lord.[1] Mary's name in Hebrew was probably the same as that of Moses' older sister, Miriam, or Miriamne, which was also the

MARY, THE MOTHER OF JESUS

name of several daughters of the royal Hasmonean family. By the first century, the name Mary was arguably the most popular name given to Jewish girls. It was the mother of Jesus, however, who gave this name a sense of awe.

In the twenty centuries since the young virgin gave birth to the Son of God, Mary has been depicted in a multiplicity of ways, giving rise to diverse traditions that have significantly influenced Christian worship among peoples all over the world. Some traditions encouraged a form of Mary worship that placed her on par with her Son as co-Redeemer. As early as the second century, Christians had begun praising her as the woman who

restored humankind from the "sin of Eve." Early church father Irenaeus (A.D. 120–202) claimed that as Eve, "having become disobedient, was made the cause of death, both to herself and to the entire human race; so also did Mary . . . by yielding obedience, become the cause of salvation, both to herself and the whole human race."[2] From that perspective, Mary was soon viewed not merely as one who had found the grace of God but as one who possessed the power to bestow such grace on others. For many early Christian writers, Mary became the model woman—docile, innocent, and unquestionably obedient to male authority.[3]

We need not worship Mary, however, to appreciate her contribution to God's work on earth. Her humble response to the angel's announcement of her role in the coming of the Son of God, "Be it unto me according to thy word," may qualify her as a pioneer Christian of the New Testament era, but it does not necessarily mean that she responded this way to anyone but God. Her realization that "all generations shall call me blessed" did not mandate her widespread worship but reflected her own sense of awe at the power of God, "for with God nothing shall be impossible" (Luke 1:38, 48, 37). Elder Bruce R. McConkie of the Quorum of the Twelve Apostles asked: "Can we speak too highly of her whom the Lord has blessed above all women? There was only one Christ, and there is only one Mary. Each was noble and great in preexistence, and each was foreordained to the ministry he or she performed."[4] Mary's conviction of God's reality and power deserves our admiration and emulation.

As widely known as the name of Mary is throughout Christendom, the New Testament and the Book of Mormon are the only authoritative sources that actually tell us much about her. This lack of information enticed many writers to fabricate stories imagining what her life should have been like to qualify her as chosen of God.

Without relying on fictional accounts, we will focus on narratives from the four New Testament Gospels and other scriptural glimpses of Mary to better know and appreciate her example. Although people naturally want more information about her and a more complete explanation of various scenes from her life than we are given, canonized scripture actually offers more insight than we often realize.

We are not usually told where the Gospel writers gleaned their information. Luke gathered much of his account through personal interviews with "eyewitnesses" (Luke 1:2), which may have included Mary herself in her later years. Any or all of the Gospel authors may also have had access to previously written accounts, such as family histories, that no longer survive.

Much has been written about the lack of agreement between Matthew's and Luke's scriptural narratives, leading some to conclude that divergent accounts were originally circulated and that both cannot be accurate. In some areas where the accounts in Matthew and in Luke invite divergent interpretations or do not intersect, another witness of Jesus

Christ—the Book of Mormon—validates, clarifies, and harmonizes the New Testament accounts. For example, the Book of Mormon tells us that Mary lived in Nazareth before Jesus was born (1 Nephi 11:13), she was a virgin (1 Nephi 11:20; Alma 7:10), she was overshadowed and conceived the Son of God by the "power of the Holy Ghost" (Alma 7:10), and Jesus was the literal son of Mary, after the manner of the flesh, and was also the very Son of God, not the offspring of the Spirit or of a mortal man (1 Nephi 11:18, 21; Mosiah 3:8).

Like many of the early Christians, we may be tempted to elaborate on the details of Mary's life in an attempt to enhance the scriptural accounts. We may cringe at the customs of her day and therefore try to synchronize them with modern-day traditions. Embellishing the accounts, however, will not bring us closer to the truths that God has set before us. By allowing the points of intersection among scriptural accounts to form the foundation of the story, we can better recognize the facts that are important, the doctrines that are then made more evident, and personal applications that are appropriate.

CHAPTER TWO

Prophecies concerning Mary

Ancient prophets spoke of Mary and of her calling as the mother of the Son of God long before she was born. The Old Testament prophet Isaiah delivered what may be the earliest prophecy of Mary, although he does not call her by name. During a military siege of Jerusalem by the combined armies of Syria and the northern kingdom of Israel (734 B.C.), Isaiah gave King Ahaz of Judah a sign that Jerusalem would be spared. The words that came from "the Lord himself" were "Behold, a virgin shall conceive, and bear a son, and shall call his name Immanuel" (Isaiah 7:14; 2 Nephi 17:14). Many scholars have discounted this as a reference to Mary because the Hebrew word translated as "virgin" here can also mean young woman or girl. When Jewish scholars later translated the Hebrew text into Greek for the Septuagint, however, they chose the Greek word *parthenos* to describe the mother, which word specifically means "virgin." Obviously, at least two hundred years before Mary gave birth to Jesus, Jewish scholars believed that Isaiah prophesied the miraculous virginal birth of "Immanuel," whose name means "God with us."

The Book of Mormon is especially rich in prophetic glimpses of Mary. While receiving instruction about his father's dream of the tree of life six hundred years before Jesus' birth, Nephi saw Mary in vision in "the city of Nazareth." She was "beautiful and fair above all other virgins" (1 Nephi 11:13, 15). The next scene again described Mary as a virgin, but this time she was cradling in her arms her newborn son, who was the Son of God (1 Nephi 11:18–20). As Jesus was represented in Lehi's dream by the tree of life, so the Father worked through Mary to give life to all his children through her son.

Some four centuries after Nephi's vision of Mary, an angel revealed to King Benjamin that "Jesus Christ, the Son of God, the Father of heaven and earth, the Creator of all things from the beginning" would come from "heaven . . . and shall dwell in a tabernacle of clay." The angel then told King Benjamin that "his mother shall be called Mary" (Mosiah 3: 8, 5, 8). Although the names of others have been specifically revealed in prophecy—such as Hannah's son Samuel and Elisabeth and Zacharias's son, John—Mary's is the only woman's name on the list. Furthermore, Mary's name was revealed more than one hundred years before her birth and to a prophet in a distant land, whereas John's and Samuel's names were revealed to their parents.

The prophet Alma taught the Nephites living in Gideon that Mary was "a virgin, a precious and chosen vessel," who would give birth to "the Son of God." He explained that this miracle would occur because she "shall be overshadowed and conceive by the power of the Holy Ghost, and bring forth a son, yea, even the Son of God" (Alma 7:10). Alma spoke of Mary's giving birth to Jesus "at Jerusalem," phraseology used by Nephite authors for the environs of a prominent city. Bethlehem was part of greater Jerusalem, being some five miles southeast of the holy city, and it therefore easily fits the description "at Jerusalem."[1]

The Book of Mormon also provides another witness for the birth of Jesus Christ. After being in a comatose state for three days, King Lamoni awoke to recount that he had seen in vision the Savior and his mother: "I have seen my Redeemer . . . born of a woman" (Alma 19:13). In learning of his redeemer, King Lamoni must have been amazed to realize that Christ would be "born of a woman." In other words, the Savior would be born into this fallen and mortal world like the rest of us. After the Savior's mortal ministry, the apostle Paul used similar terminology when he spoke of the miraculous birth of Christ: "God sent forth his Son, made of a woman" (Galatians 4:5).

Without question, the primary purposes and the main focus of revelation from ancient prophets were related to the coming of a redeemer who would be the Son of God. This savior's coming, however, could not be fully understood or appreciated without knowing about his mother. These prophecies never confused the Savior's mother with deity: she would be a mortal from among the multitude of God's people. Notwithstanding, this mother was not Any Woman; she was chosen and known by name centuries before her birth. Clearly, God intended us to know about her and her contribution to his plan of salvation.

CHAPTER THREE

CHILDHOOD OF JEWISH GIRLS

Philo (ca. 20 B.C.–A.D. 50), a well-educated Jew and contemporary of Mary, wrote much about Judaism during the Hellenistic era from his home in Alexandria, Egypt. He had strong opinions about young daughters, whom he viewed as a constant danger to a family's reputation should they be found unchaste when they married. Consequently, for modesty's sake, according to Philo, they should rarely leave their homes. Philo considered unmarried daughters brazen if they intermingled with men in the streets like common trollops. He wrote: "Taking care of the house and remaining at home are the proper duties of women; the virgins having their apartments in the centre of the house within the innermost doors, and the full-grown women not going beyond the vestibule and outer courts. . . . Let no woman busy herself about those things which are beyond the province of [economy], but let her cultivate solitude, and not be seen to be going about like a woman who walks the streets in the sight of other men, except when it is necessary for her to go to the temple, if she has any proper regard for herself; and even then let her not go at noon when the market is full, but after the greater part of the people have returned home; like a well-born woman."[1]

Philo's description of proper decorum for women presupposes wealth, a large home with multiple rooms and courts, and servants to go to the marketplace to accomplish the errands necessary to run a household. Mary's life in little Nazareth of Galilee, however, does not fit Philo's portrayal of childhood for a well-born Jewish girl.

Far from any urban center and families of elite social status, parents in Nazareth could not have afforded to keep their daughters in seclusion.[2] Their girls would more likely have been involved in assisting with the family vocation, whether farming, raising livestock, creating stone masonry, pottery, or textiles, or selling such goods. Daughters would have also assisted their mothers in preparing food and caring for the home. Praising rural women in the Roman Empire generally, the Roman scholar Varro (116 B.C.–27 B.C.) reported that their fortitude and usefulness put to shame the pampered women in the cities. One scholar noted of Varro: "He describes those women who look after the herdsmen watching the livestock in the mountains, claiming that the women are often not at all inferior to the men in working with the flocks. Not only can they look after the animals, but they can also cook food and keep the huts clean. And they do this all with nursing babies at their breast!"[3]

A further indication that Mary's world differed from the one described by Philo is that after the angel's annunciation to her in Nazareth, she traveled to visit Elisabeth outside Jerusalem, a multiple days' journey (Luke 1:36–39). Because traveling alone was deemed imprudent for anyone, including men, she must have been accompanied by others. But her decision to leave her house and town does not seem to have raised eyebrows. When the angel informed her of Elisabeth's condition and implied that Mary should visit her, Mary expressed no concern over being away from home for three months (Luke 1:39–56).

Considering the potential all children had to contribute to a family's livelihood, some first-century families valued their daughters as much as their sons. Furthermore, whomever a daughter attracted as a marriage partner could significantly affect the family's social prestige. A girl's status as unmarried may have been indicated by specific clothing. For example, she may have worn a distinctive veil such as Rebekah wore before she met Isaac (Genesis 24:65). The apocryphal story of Aseneth, the bride of Joseph who was sold into Egypt, indicates that virgins wore a second sash, or girdle, to distinguish them from other women. All women wore the first sash around the waist, but virgins may have worn an additional sash under or over the breast.[4] When a daughter followed social norms, behaved modestly, and worked hard, she would be a source of pride for the family and advance the family honor. The scant information we have about Mary in the New

Testament indicates that she was a model daughter. After all, the angel told her that she was "highly favoured" by God (Luke 1:28).

Six centuries earlier, Nephi saw Mary in vision and described her as "most beautiful and fair above all other virgins" (1 Nephi 11:15). Because qualifications for beauty are often cultural and have differed over time, we may wonder whether Nephi was noting Mary's physical characteristics or her purity, goodness, and diligence—or all of those attributes. That the vision first focused on Mary herself, before she gave birth to Jesus, indicates that she was important to God as a precious daughter, apart from her role as the mother of his Son.

During her childhood, Mary would likely have been taught to work and in other ways to prepare for marriage and motherhood. Her mother would have been her most important teacher. Because no reputable ancient record preserves anything about her life or her family before the angel Gabriel appeared to her in Nazareth, we therefore assume Mary's was a typical life for a Jewish girl. We wonder, however, if while she worked in and around her family's home, she received any premonition or spiritual preparation for the God-given assignment that would be hers.

CHAPTER FOUR

Jewish Marriage Customs

At Mary's introduction in the Gospel of Matthew, she was "espoused" to be married to Joseph (Matthew 1:18). The Jewish marriage procedure in her day consisted of two ceremonies that usually took place a year or more apart, one before puberty and the other afterward: (1) the legally binding contract of marriage signed before witnesses (Malachi 2:14), and later (2) the consummation of the marriage and relocation of the bride to live in the husband's home, as portrayed in the parable of the ten virgins (Matthew 25:1–13). According to the Mishnah (the ancient Jewish oral law as it was written in A.D. 200), a girl was considered a minor when she was younger than twelve years old, of age to marry between twelve and twelve-and-a-half years, and "past her girlhood" when she was older than twelve-and-a-half years.[1] A young man was deemed "fit" for the "bride-chamber" at eighteen years of age.[2] In part because of the youthfulness of the couple, parents played a prominent role in selecting marriage partners for their children. The families were therefore often well acquainted before the marriage, and even more often they were related, as will be discussed below in the case of Mary and Joseph.

The first step in the marriage procedure was a legal agreement established before witnesses in which the men of the bride's and groom's families formally consented to join their families through this marriage. This event was likely accompanied by a meal served at the bride's father's home.[3] The Hebrew term for the consent phase is often translated as "betrothal" or "espousal," but it constituted a legal marriage in that the young woman was permanently bound to the young man. In other words, it was not simply an engagement in the way we use that term today. Any compromise of the groom's marital rights over the young woman made her liable to being legally punished for adultery. Although the bride continued to live in her father's home until the second part of the marriage procedure was accomplished, she was the "wife" of her betrothed. The Mishnah states that at the time of "betrothal," the bride "enters into the control of the husband" in place of her father, which includes "the right to set aside her vows" with a "bill of divorce."[4] Thus, Joseph would have had to obtain a divorce to be released from his obligation to Mary (Matthew 1:19).

The second stage of the marriage procedure occurred after the husband established a home for his wife and future family, usually in his parents' home. Matthew 25:1–13 describes this event, in which the virgin bride waits at her home for the bridegroom's formal arrival to take her to his home, where he will assume full responsibility for her support. In the Greco-Roman period, the era in which Mary lived, the bride wore a veil that was "apparently the color of flame, a bright yellow or orange. After [relocating to her husband's home], the bride, now a matron, wore a *stola* (a sleeveless dress over her tunic) and a *palla*, a rectangular cloth that she wrapped around her shoulders and could pull up to cover her head."[5] Now a member of her husband's family, the teenage wife would typically be instructed in her new role by her mother-in-law. The transition could be very difficult for the young bride, considering the potentially strange and even hostile new surroundings to which she was expected to quickly adapt.[6]

According to Matthew's account, Joseph and Mary had completed the first part of the marriage—the contract and vows—but had not yet consummated the marriage (Matthew 1:18). Therefore, when Joseph learned that Mary was pregnant and not by him, the natural assumption was that she had engaged in adulterous behavior and was subject to legal consequences (Deuteronomy 22:21–22). We are told that Mary was not guilty of sin, that she was with child through the power of the Holy Ghost, but Joseph had not yet been informed of that, so he planned to terminate the previous espousal agreement.

CHAPTER FIVE

The Annunciation in Nazareth

The only domestic background we are given for Mary comes from Luke's Gospel. There we learn that she lived in Nazareth, "had found favour with God," and was a virgin, because she "[knew] not a man" sexually (Luke 1:30, 34).

Nazareth is situated about fifteen miles west of the Sea of Galilee and twenty miles from the Mediterranean Sea. At the beginning of the first century, the town likely covered no more than sixty acres and sustained a population of some 480 inhabitants.[1] Most likely, Mary's home with her parents in Nazareth would have been small and unassuming, much like the other homes in the vicinity.

Luke's narrative reads, "And in the sixth month the angel Gabriel was sent from God unto a city of Galilee, named Nazareth," where he appeared to the virgin Mary (Luke 1:26). The "sixth month" refers not to the month of the year but to the month of

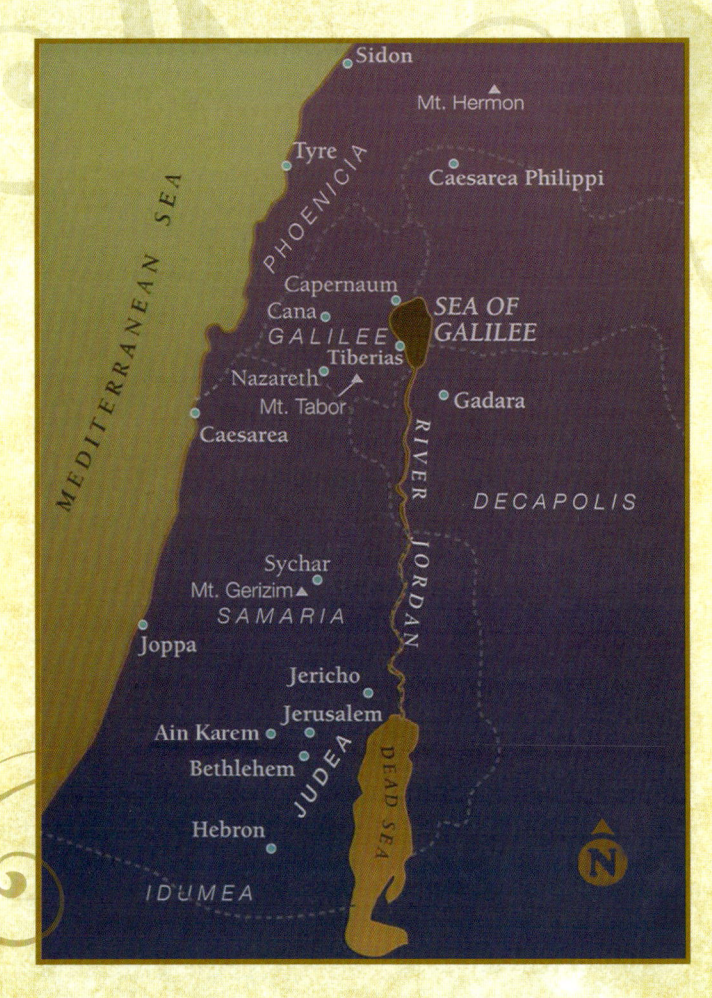

Elisabeth's pregnancy. In other words, when Elisabeth, wife of Zacharias, was in her sixth month of pregnancy, Gabriel visited Mary to announce the coming of Jesus.

Only two other accounts of an angel appearing to a woman are recorded in the Bible, and both times the visit was to announce that the woman would soon give birth to a son. The earliest of these recorded appearances was to Hagar, the mother of Ishmael (Genesis 16:7–11), and the other was to the mother of Samson (Judges 13:3). Jewish girls did not likely anticipate such angelic communications.

Although Matthew says nothing about Mary living in Nazareth before the birth of Jesus, Nephi saw her in Nazareth as a young woman before becoming a mother, exactly as Luke recounted (1 Nephi 11:13).

We are not told whether Joseph also resided in Nazareth at that time. It is possible that he did, if only because he was a descendant of David. Historical evidence shows that some Davidic families relocated to Galilee from their ancestral homes in Judea, likely to avoid attention from Hasmonean leaders who feared competition for the throne of the Judean kingdom.[2] Or Joseph may have lived in Bethlehem and gone to Nazareth only when it was time to take his espoused wife home. Considering how long the holy family remained in Bethlehem after Jesus was born gives further credence to this suggestion. Regardless of Joseph's origins, the couple were likely not well acquainted with each other before they began living together.

When Gabriel, whom Joseph Smith identified as the Old Testament prophet

Noah,³ appeared to Mary, he calmed her "troubled," or startled, heart with "Fear not, Mary: for thou hast found favour with [or received grace from] God" (Luke 1:29–30). In contrast to this glorious angel and the immortal Being he represented, the mortal Mary acknowledged great wonderment that the Lord knew her name and so favored her.

Gabriel then proclaimed the holy words: "Thou shalt conceive in thy womb, and bring forth a son, and shalt call his name Jesus. He shall be great, and shall be called the Son of the Highest: and the Lord God shall give unto him the throne of his father David: And he shall reign over the house of Jacob for ever; and of his kingdom there shall be no end" (Luke 1:31–33).

The announcement was to Mary

alone, emphasized by the angel's use of the second person singular. In today's vernacular, Gabriel said, *You* will conceive . . . *you* will bear . . . and *you* will name . . .[4]

Mary apparently showed no concern over how she would bear a child who could inherit the throne of David but only over how she could bear a child because she was a virgin. That she was a descendant of David could explain how her child would inherit the requisite lineage; her concern was, therefore, "How shall this be, seeing I know not a man?" (Luke 1:34). How could a virgin give birth?

One purpose of Gabriel's annunciation was to communicate how the seemingly impossible can indeed happen but only through the grace or gift of God. Similar to what the prophet Alma learned through revelation, the angel explained to Mary how she would conceive this chosen Son: "The Holy Ghost shall come upon thee, and the power of the Highest shall overshadow thee: therefore also that holy thing which shall be born of thee shall be called the Son of God" (Luke 1:35; see also Alma 7:10; JST, Luke 1:35). The Greek words translated as "the power of the Highest shall overshadow thee" do not imply a sexual union. In fact, Luke uses the same term translated "overshadowed" to describe Peter, James, and John on the Mount of Transfiguration (Luke 9:34) and also Peter's shadow healing the sick as he passed by them (Acts 5:15).

In Matthew's Gospel, the angel explained to Joseph that "that which is conceived in her is of the Holy Ghost" (Matthew 1:20). We know that by the power of the Holy Ghost, Mary was enabled miraculously to conceive God's son, "the Son of the Highest," in her womb (Luke 1:32). Latter-day scripture clarifies that no man or woman "can see the face of God, even the Father, and live," without the "power of godliness" and "the authority of the priesthood" (D&C 84:22, 21). Without question, Mary experienced a miracle: "He that is mighty hath done to me great things; and holy is his name" (Luke 1:49), but we are not justified in speculating further.

As the only mortal participant in this unique miracle, Mary reported no other details, which testifies of her reverence for the sacred event. Her foreordained mission, as important as it was, did not include a detailed account of the great condescension of God—how he descended from his glorious state to live among mortals in a fallen world. Rather than through a testimonial of words, Mary proclaimed her faith in God through her actions in choosing to obey his will. Demonstrating true discipleship, she responded to the angel's announcement with the words, "Behold the handmaid of the Lord; be it unto me according to thy word" (Luke 1:38). The word translated here as "handmaid" is the feminine form of "servant" (or possibly even "slave"). She had not chosen this assignment but quickly accepted it, reverencing God's authority without question, even though at that moment she could not have completely understood all that was said and done nor the challenges that awaited her.

Elder James E. Talmage of the Quorum of the Twelve Apostles observed of Gabriel's visit to Mary: "True, the event was unprecedented; true also it has never been paralleled; but that the virgin birth would be unique was as truly essential to the fulfilment of

THE ANNUNCIATION IN NAZARETH

prophecy as that it should occur at all. That Child to be born of Mary was begotten of Elohim, the Eternal Father, not in violation of natural law but in accordance with a higher manifestation thereof."[5]

Mary's expression "be it unto me" is in the form of a prayer, such as "may this occur to me as thou hast declared." Her desire to obey God was not merely mechanical or dutiful but almost enthusiastic. Without hesitation, Mary lived her faith in God. "What Mary brought to God's plan of salvation was her faith that the creator God could accomplish this [the conception of his Only Begotten Son]."[6]

be it unto me

CHAPTER SIX

JOSEPH

The scriptures do not tell us how Joseph learned that his betrothed was carrying a child. We know only that Joseph knew Mary was pregnant and that he was not the father of her child, because her pregnancy occurred "before they came together." He therefore planned to "put her away privily" (Matthew 1:18–19). Under the law of Moses, if a woman was found not to be a virgin at marriage, she could be stoned to death (Deuteronomy 22:21). It is not certain whether the Mosaic law was applied strictly enough in Galilee in the first century so that Mary's life was truly in danger, but at the very least, her reputation would have been damaged if her condition was made public.[1]

Born into the tribe of Judah and a descendant of King David, Joseph is described as a "just" or upright man (Matthew 1:19). In contrast to others in his Davidic genealogy listed in the first verses of Matthew 1—men such as Judah, David, and Manasseh—Joseph is portrayed as being particularly observant of the law. But Joseph was more than upright. He was also merciful. His strict obedience to the law did not preclude him from showing compassion toward Mary and resisting an opportunity to expose her "sin" publicly.

His compassion, however, it did not extend to completing the marriage contract and taking his pregnant bride into his home. Joseph's uprightness in the law precluded his seeing any option but divorce, even a private one. Because Jewish law in that day required a man who wished to put away his wife to denounce her before two or three witnesses in order to receive a legal writ of repudiation (Matthew 19:7), knowledge of the reason for the divorce could not have been kept secret. Moreover, in only a few months, Mary's pregnancy would have been impossible to hide and would likely have become the subject of small-town accusations and scorn. Most likely, the act of "put[ting] her away privily" (Matthew 1:19) meant that Joseph would not bring criminal charges of adultery against Mary nor repudiate her publicly, thereby subjecting her to as little ugliness in the process as possible.[2]

Such was Joseph's intent as "he thought on these things" (Matthew 1:20), perhaps hoping for another option, when his pondering gave rise to a vision in which an angel appeared with a message from God. That Joseph was sufficiently in tune with the Spirit to receive such a revelation is again evidence of his obedience to God's word and of his merciful regard toward Mary. He was steadfastly prepared to obey what he understood to be God's will until the Lord gave him further instruction. Then the angel announced, "Joseph, thou son of David, fear not to take unto thee Mary thy wife: for that which is conceived in her is of the Holy Ghost. And she shall bring forth a son, and thou shalt call his name Jesus: for he shall save his people from their sins" (Matthew 1:20–21).

It is significant that Mary did not reveal to Joseph the sacred truth of the origin of her unborn child, which could easily have been justified in her precarious situation. She was not commissioned to proclaim the paternity of her child. Even though she did not understand all the ramifications of God's work through her, she "kept all these sayings in her heart" (Luke 2:19). She kept sacred things sacred, even when, as far as she could tell, her reputation and future were clearly in jeopardy. It took the visit of an angel to Joseph in a dream to vindicate Mary's character and give him God's directive to complete his marriage to Mary by taking her to live with him in his house. Furthermore, in the vision Joseph learned that the child's name would be Jesus, a Hellenized form of the Hebrew *Yeshua* (Joshua), meaning "Jehovah helps," or as the angel observed, "Jehovah saves."

In his Gospel, Matthew cites Isaiah's extraordinary prophecy concerning Mary: "Behold, a virgin shall conceive, and bear a son, and shall call his name Immanuel" (Isaiah 7:14). This prophecy shed further light on the identity of the baby. Not only did the name of Mary's unborn child declare that Jehovah saves but in her womb she carried that very Jehovah, even Emmanuel, or "God with us" (Matthew 1:23). Through Mary, the Son of God—he whom the Israelites knew as Jehovah—would be born to live among mortals in a fallen world. Thus the angel declared to Nephi in a vision of the Savior's birth, "Behold the condescension of God!" (1 Nephi 11:26).

CHAPTER SEVEN

MARY'S LINEAGE

According to Jewish custom in Mary's day, genealogy was traced through the father rather than the mother. That tradition is illustrated in both genealogies of Jesus found in the Gospels, tracing Joseph's lineage rather than Mary's, as though Jesus were Joseph's biological son (Matthew 1:16; Luke 3:23). Similarly, both Matthew and Luke identify Joseph as being of the tribe of Judah and a descendant of King David; they do not mention Mary's parentage (Matthew 1:20; Luke 2:4).

The scriptures are equally clear that Joseph was not Jesus' literal father but only his legal father. Of foundational importance throughout scripture is the truth that Jesus is literally God's Begotten Son, not the son of a mortal man. Peter testified that Jesus was "the Son of the living God" and was immeasurably blessed for achieving this knowledge (Matthew 16:16). John specifically identified Jesus as "the only begotten of the Father"

(John 1:14; 3:16). Paul declared, "God [sent] his own Son in the likeness of sinful flesh" and "[God] spared not his own Son, but delivered him up for us all" (Romans 8:3, 32).

The truth about the Savior's divine parentage is likewise underscored in the other standard works, including his own declaration to the Nephites: "Behold, I am Jesus Christ the Son of God. I created the heavens and the earth, and all things that in them are. I was with the Father from the beginning. I am in the Father, and the Father in me; and in me hath the Father glorified his name" (3 Nephi 9:15). Furthermore, Jesus' coming, his name, and his relationship to the Father as "the Son of God" were known centuries before Mary gave birth to him (2 Nephi 25:19). In considering the genealogies of Jesus in the New Testament, we cannot equivocate on this truth: Jesus was not the Son of the Spirit or of Joseph or of any other mortal man. Jesus was the biological Son of God.

With equal certainty, we must conclude that Jesus was the son of Mary. He inherited mortal qualities from her that allowed him to feel hunger, thirst, pain, and even death. These attributes were essential to allow him to be "filled with mercy" and "know . . . how to succor his people according to their infirmities" (Alma 7:11–12). Through Mary, he became mortal so that he could lay down his life as a sacrifice for sin (Mosiah 15:5–8; Hebrews 2:9, 17–18).

God revealed through Old Testament prophets that his Son would be born into the lineage of the Israelite kings. Beginning with Jacob's blessing to his son Judah, we see God's foreknowledge of those who would provide the lineage of his Son:

- "The sceptre shall not depart from Judah, nor a lawgiver from between his feet, until Shiloh come" (Genesis 49:10). In Joseph Smith's translation (JST) of Genesis 50:24, "Shiloh" is identified as the Messiah.

- Through the prophet Nathan, God renewed his promise to David, a descendant of Judah, saying, "I will set up thy seed after thee, . . . and I will stablish the throne of his kingdom for ever. I will be his father, and he shall be my son" (2 Samuel 7:12–14).

- "The Lord hath sworn in truth unto David; . . . of the fruit of thy body will I set upon thy throne" (Psalm 132:11).

- Isaiah prophesied of the "stem of Jesse" (Isaiah 11:1). Jesse was the father of David, and through modern revelation we know that the "stem" is Jesus Christ (D&C 113:1–2). In other words, Jesus Christ is descended from Jesse and David.

- Speaking for the Lord, Jeremiah foretold, "I will raise unto David a righteous Branch, . . . and this is the name whereby he shall be called, THE LORD OUR RIGHTEOUSNESS" (Jeremiah 23:5–6).

Other scriptural passages indicate that first-century Jews understood testimonies that prophesied that God's Son would be born into David's lineage. For example, consider these three passages:

- Jews debating whether Jesus could be the Christ said, "Hath not the scripture said, That Christ cometh of the seed of David, and out of the town of Bethlehem, where David was?" (John 7:42).

- Peter reminded the Jews of the oath God had made to their father David that "of the fruit of his loins, according to the flesh, he [God] would raise up Christ to sit on his throne" (Acts 2:30).

- Likewise the apostle Paul taught Jews during his first mission, "Of this man's [David's] seed hath God according to his promise raised unto Israel a Saviour, Jesus" (Acts 13:23).

These prophecies and the way the Jews understood them in Jesus' day clearly indicate that Jesus would be born through David's lineage. True, under Jewish law an adopted child had all the rights and identity of his adopted father, so Jesus could legally claim Davidic descent from Joseph even though Joseph was not his biological father. But is that what God and his prophets foresaw? Were prophets speaking of Jesus as an adopted son of David rather than a biological son? Or was Jesus a literal, biological descendant of the royal Israelite lineage from the tribe of Judah through David? If he was the literal seed of David and not merely a legal heir, then Mary must also be of Davidic lineage; through Mary, Jesus would then receive his prophetically designated genealogy.

Certain verses of scripture indicate that Mary inherited royal blood. When Gabriel announced to her that she would conceive a child in her womb who would be given "the throne of his father David" (Luke 1:32), Mary did not protest that because she did not descend through that lineage, how could her son? Neither did she think about someone else who could supply that legacy for her son—the Davidic Joseph, for example. The only deterrent to her ability to bear a son with royal lineage was the existence of the requisite man in the equation: "How shall this be, seeing I know not a man" (Luke 1:34). Her statement may argue that she could provide the Davidic lineage, regardless of who the man was.

The apostle Paul spoke of the Savior in terms that make it impossible to deny Mary's Davidic lineage. Speaking in past tense and thereby not by prophecy but by accomplished fact, Paul wrote "concerning [God's] Son Jesus Christ our Lord, which was made of the seed of David according to the flesh" (Romans 1:3). The term "according to the flesh" indicates literal, not adoptive, lineage. In his final epistle, Paul again wrote of "Jesus

Christ of the seed of David was raised from the dead" (2 Timothy 2:8). Latter-day apostle Elder James E. Talmage also said that Mary was a descendant of David: "In common with other daughters of Israel, specifically those of the tribe of Judah and of known descent from David, Mary had doubtless contemplated . . . the coming of the Messiah through the royal line; she knew that some Jewish maiden was yet to become the mother of the Christ."[1]

When we compare Luke's narrative of John the Baptist's parentage to that of Jesus, another argument for Mary's Davidic lineage emerges. To anticipate the miracles surrounding Mary's virginal conception of Jesus, Luke introduces his readers to the story of John the Baptist as a type, or shadow, of Mary's story, although not quite as miraculous. The lineage of John was as important for his mission as Jesus' lineage was for him. Even though Levite men were expected to marry women from their same tribe, Luke notes not only Zacharias's lineage but also that of his wife, Elisabeth. Both were of the tribe of Levi and descended also through Aaron, making their son a priest like Zacharias (Luke 1:5). The parallel to the story it typifies is that both Mary and Joseph were likewise of the tribe of Judah and descended from David. Some scholars have suggested that Jesus was sometimes called "son of Mary" rather than the expected "son of Joseph" because she came from a family of higher social standing than he did.[2]

Consideration of Mary's lineage must also take into account Luke's observation that she was a "cousin" to Elisabeth (Luke 1:36). What can we understand from indications that Mary had lineage through the royal line of Judah but was also related to Elisabeth, who is descended from Levi, the lineage of priesthood? Perhaps Mary's father was of Judah and her mother was of Levi. Her son could therefore possess blood inheritance to qualify as literally the King of Kings and the great High Priest.

Just as Mary was chosen to be the mother of God's Son long before she was born, so God orchestrated her lineage. Her genealogy is not preserved in scripture, but the necessary lineal criteria for Mary are found in scripture. If indeed Jesus needed a biological connection to both the royal and priestly lineages, it is highly possible that Mary could have provided them. At various times Jesus was called the Prophet, Priest, and King. Because of Mary's lineage, those titles could be not merely legal but literal. Because of the Father, the Savior's titles are eternal.

CHAPTER EIGHT

Mary's Visit to Elisabeth

Before the angel Gabriel departed from Mary in Nazareth, he gave her a sign that certainly must have bolstered her faith and given her comfort after his life-changing announcement. Six months previously, her relative Elisabeth, who lived in Judea, had also conceived a son, even though "in her old age . . . [she] was called barren" (Luke 1:36). Because Elisabeth hid herself away during her pregnancy, probably out of modesty, few if any besides Zacharias would have been aware of her good news (Luke 1:24). The text of Luke suggests that soon after the annunciation and conception, Mary left home to visit Elisabeth "in those days" and went "with haste" to the city in Judea where Elisabeth lived with Zacharias (Luke 1:39). Her prompt departure reveals her complete commitment to God's plan rather than fear of what others may say or do should her secret be known.

Likely no one else was aware that Mary was pregnant, including Joseph, when she set off for the Judean hill country. Because solitary travel was unsafe and therefore imprudent, women did not travel alone in first-century Palestine. Although the scriptural text is silent concerning traveling partners, Mary would almost assuredly have made the journey in the company of others. The traditional location of Elisabeth and Zacharias's home is Ain Karem, a town about five miles west of Jerusalem. If Mary's journey commenced in Nazareth, as Luke chronicles, she traveled close to one hundred miles, which would have taken approximately five days.[1]

Visualizing Mary and Elisabeth together illustrates the unique parallels and stark contrasts in their personal experiences. The Bible rarely preserves dialogue between two women, and in this case, no one else was around. No other event, conversation, or experience anywhere else in the world at that moment was as important as this one. Heaven's spotlight was focused squarely on two women—one elderly and the other very young—carrying within them "the hopes and fears of all the years."[2]

The central focus of this event is Mary and Elisabeth's double witness of the divinity of Mary's unborn Son. Considering other biblical stories that feature two women, we might anticipate potential competition, jealousy, or conflict, as may be seen between Sarah and Hagar, Leah and Rachel, Hannah and Penninah, and the New Testament Mary and Martha. Nevertheless, like Ruth and Naomi, Mary and Elisabeth epitomized mutual respect, cooperation, and an understanding and reverence for the grace of God that surrounded them.

MARY'S VISIT TO ELISABETH

Nothing suggests that Elisabeth was expecting a visit from Mary, let alone that Elisabeth guessed anything that had happened to Mary in Nazareth. But as soon as she saw Mary enter her home and heard her greeting, Elisabeth knew all the essential truths. "When Elisabeth heard the salutation of Mary, the babe [John the Baptist] leaped in her womb; and Elisabeth was filled with the Holy Ghost" (Luke 1:41). In a dramatic and personal manner, God revealed to this priestly woman the secret of the ages.

Notice that Mary did not utter these truths—all was communicated through the Spirit to Elisabeth, who then gave it voice. "For, lo," Elisabeth exclaimed to Mary, "as soon as the voice of thy salutation sounded in mine ears, the babe leaped in my womb for joy" (Luke 1:44). God gave each of these women a clear revelation of what he had done for the other; neither could have known of the other's condition without God's communication.

Although Mary would not yet have been showing any physical signs of pregnancy, Elisabeth knew immediately that she was carrying a child. More importantly, where

Elisabeth's natural response to that information alone might be to feel shame or at least embarrassment for Mary, instead, Elisabeth praised her! In words that have been called a hymn, or canticle, Elisabeth testified, "Blessed art thou among women, and blessed is the fruit of thy womb. And whence is this to me, that the mother of my Lord should come to me?" (Luke 1:42–43).

Understandably, Elisabeth might have been more in awe of her own miraculous pregnancy in comparison with all the younger mothers-to-be around her, yet she was clearly aware that the "fruit" of Mary's womb was infinitely greater even than her own. Furthermore, she was ecstatic to confess it aloud. As miraculous as Elisabeth's pregnancy was after years of barrenness, Mary had conceived a child without "knowing" a man, a phenomenon that was exponentially more astonishing. Mary's child was "totally God's work—a new creation."[3] And in that instant, Elisabeth realized it. She knew that Mary would give birth to him who had the power to save her as she declared Mary's child not as merely *the* Lord but "*my* Lord" (Luke 1:43).

Elisabeth praised Mary: "Blessed art thou among women." This was not a prayer to Mary but the recognition of a blessing God had already bestowed upon her. Concerning Elisabeth's comparison of Mary "among women," scholar Raymond Brown explained, "This phrase has a comparative (but not an absolutely superlative) value both in Greek and in Hebrew. It means that Mary has been specially blessed by God, but not necessarily that she is the most blessed woman."[4] Yes, God blessed Mary in a unique way—but he did not love and bless Mary more than he loves and blesses any other woman. In truth, the accounts of both Mary and Elisabeth show us that God bestows gifts on each of us individually.

With striking humility considering her own private miracle, Elisabeth sincerely wondered, "Who am I to receive a visit from the mother of my Savior?" Through the Spirit and in an instant, she knew that God had engaged Mary in his plan of salvation.

In this sacred setting, Mary then burst into her own praise for God in a canticle known in Latin as the Magnificat. Many scholars today think that the Magnificat did not originate with Mary, suggesting that the words fit Elisabeth's position better than they fit Mary's, or that the hymn was already widely known at the time and Luke simply attributed it to Mary in his narrative.[5] Whatever the true origin, the words of the Magnificat can be seen to resonate with Mary's state at that moment of greeting Elisabeth. Even if she was not the first to utter these lines, she did link them to her life and thereby offered them the application so meaningful to us.

The Magnificat deserves particular attention here as each line underscores how God's goodness and power are magnified through Mary's and Elisabeth's experiences.

Blessed art thou AMONG WOMEN

*My soul doth magnify the Lord
And my spirit hath rejoiced in God my Saviour.
For he hath regarded the low estate of his handmaiden:
    For, behold, from henceforth all generations
    shall call me blessed.
For he that is mighty hath done to me great things;
    And holy is his name.
And his mercy is on them that fear him
    From generation to generation.
He hath [shown] strength with his arm;
    He hath scattered the proud in the imagination
    of their hearts.
He hath put down the mighty from their seats,
    And exalted them of low degree.
He hath filled the hungry with good things;
    And the rich he hath sent empty away.
He hath holpen his servant Israel,
    In remembrance of his mercy;
As he spake to our fathers,
    To Abraham, and to his seed for ever.*

Luke 1:46–55

The first two lines portray three sets of parallels: "soul" and "spirit" are used identically, "magnify" is echoed in "rejoiced," and "the Lord" is identified as "God my Saviour." Through Mary's jubilant spirit, the greatness of the Lord God is magnified. She will forever stand as a witness of God's miraculous goodness and power.

God noticed the "low estate" of his handmaiden (literally, a female domestic servant or slave). Reproach and low estate reflect the Jewish perception of women who were barren. Elisabeth's childlessness and consequent "reproach among men" for so many years are also reflected here (Luke 1:25). The phrase may additionally point to the potential for scandal surrounding Mary's pregnancy, putting her in a "low estate." But Mary may have intended something simpler. She was part of a minority society within the Roman Empire. In her own Jewish culture, women were viewed as being less than men. Yet within her own society, she was noticed and singled out for a glorious mission by her "Saviour." Only one woman in the history of the world would receive such a call, and God chose and graced Mary. Her deep humility was not lessened by her astounding realization that "all generations will call me blessed." She was blessed because of her willing obedience and because of God's abundant gift.

The remainder of the hymn celebrates the power of God given to all those who hunger and thirst after righteousness. Through his might, the Lord accomplishes miracles and showers "mercy," or unmerited loving-kindness, upon those who "fear him," or honor, revere, and feel intense awe for him. Certainly, "Holy is his name."

Considering that "hath shewed strength" literally translates to "hath made strength,"[6] it is apparent that God *makes* those who fear him strong enough to surmount whatever he requires. By contrast, those who fear not God, or "the proud," are left to flounder, being guided only by their imaginations.

With his infinite wisdom and power, God pulls down the earthly "mighty," the princes of this world, and elevates the good people of no social or political status. Like Mary and Elisabeth, good women everywhere are "exalted" from the "low degree" in which the world sees them, not through the efforts of the so-called mighty but through the power of the one and only Almighty.

In a parallel comparison to the preceding verse, verse 53 states that through God's almighty power and mercy, the wicked wealthy will find themselves impoverished, or "empty," and those who are "hungry" for righteousness will be filled with an abundance of "good things."

The Greek word here translated "holpen" means more than merely "helped." The verb implies "taking hold in order to support."[7] Mary's canticle reminds Israel that God has taken Abraham's descendants by the hand, as manifest by his constant gift of mercy. The great extent of God's "help" is identified in the next verse. In the magnificent Abrahamic covenant, God vowed to speak to Abraham, Isaac, and Jacob forever through direct revelation and promised their descendants his gospel and the opportunity to spread it to all the families of the earth (Abraham 2:9–11).

As does Hannah's psalm in 1 Samuel 2:1–10, Mary's canticle recognizes the wonder of God, who works reversals in our lives. While the rich and powerful will encounter frustration and disappointment, the poor and lowly will become the spiritually wealthy and great. Mary's recitation of this fact also portrays her as an interpreter of the gospel. Moved by the Holy Spirit, she bears witness of truths that have not yet occurred as though they were an accomplished fact. In her Magnificat, Mary exemplifies what it means to have "the spirit of prophecy" (Revelation 19:10). When we consider her exchange with Elisabeth, we marvel even more at the depth of Mary's faith, courage, and maturity at such a young age.

Luke tells us that Mary remained with Elisabeth for the final three months of the latter's pregnancy before returning to "her own house" in Nazareth; in other words, she had not yet moved into Joseph's house (Luke 1:56). No doubt, then, she was with Elisabeth for the birth of John before she returned. In his narrative, Luke completes his account of Mary's actions in this segment with verse 55 before bringing to conclusion Zacharias and Elisabeth's story in verses 56–80, and so his narrative should not be viewed as strictly chronological. In addition to helping Elisabeth at John's birth, the time Mary spent with Elisabeth would have been most educational in preparing for her own delivery. No mention is made of Mary's own mother, but we may surmise from this scene that Elisabeth is certainly a mother figure in Mary's life.

CHAPTER NINE

Jesus' Birth in Bethlehem

Time markers from various primary sources indicate that Mary probably gave birth to the Son of God before 2 B.C.[1] Although at first it might seem obvious that Jesus was born in the "year of the Lord," or *anno domini* (A.D. 1), our present calendar is inaccurate. The seeming contradiction of dating Jesus' birth to years B.C. ("before Christ") is explained by mistakes made in developing a dating system centuries after the Savior's mortal life. Specifically, at the behest of Christians in the sixth century, a Scythian monk named Dionysius Exiguus invented a calendar that reckoned time from the year that Jesus was born rather than from the era of the Roman emperor Diocletian (A.D. 284–305). Unfortunately, Dionysius made some miscalculations.

To compound the confusion surrounding the precise date of Jesus' birth, there is an apparent lack of consensus among reputable primary sources as well as an absence of any mention of Jesus in first-century historical records outside the New Testament. All these circumstances indicate that our calculations must be somewhat fluid. For our purposes here, we consider that Jesus was born sometime around 6 B.C to 2 B.C.

Luke recorded that everyone went "into his own city" to be taxed, according to a government decree made some time before Mary was to give birth (Luke 2:1–3). From verse 4 of Luke's account, we know that Joseph's own city was Bethlehem, "because he was of the house and lineage of David," and Bethlehem was David's city. The census was specifically linked to ancestry because recording people by families made the count more accurate. Later, Luke observes that Joseph *and* Mary's "own city" was Nazareth (Luke 2:39). The earlier use of "own city" may refer to place of ancestral origin, whereas the second instance refers to place of current residence. Interestingly, an ancient Greek manuscript of the Gospel of Luke changes the wording in verse 4 to read, "*They* were of the house and lineage of David."[2] Although this is the sole instance of this variant reading of Luke and thereafter the word *they* was corrected to *he,* we may consider that at least one early Christian scholar recognized that Mary was a descendant of David.

In setting the scene for the birth of Christ, Luke shows us that in the midst of a powerful empire with authority to control the people by relocating and counting every individual in the land, "the seemingly ordinary, insignificant Mary gives birth to her seemingly ordinary, insignificant baby," whose power and authority supersedes them all.[3] With the political powers oblivious to the long-awaited miracle at their door, "unto us a child is born, unto us a son is given: and the government shall be upon *his* shoulder: and his name shall be called Wonderful, Counsellor, The mighty God, The everlasting Father, The Prince of Peace" (Isaiah 9:6; emphasis added). Isaiah's prophecy resonates because the babe born in Bethlehem will ultimately be recognized as the true King. With eyes of faith, we can see him as such, even during his mortal ministry amid the so-called powerful rulers, and we respond with profound reverence because we know who he really is.

The Judean town of Bethlehem is located about five miles southeast of Jerusalem. Because the time of Passover was also at hand, the city of Jerusalem and its environs would have been crowded with the Jewish faithful who came to worship at the temple, as required by law. This picture of an overcrowded Jerusalem that spilled into such nearby villages as Bethlehem makes clear Luke's observation that "there was no room for them in the inns" (JST, Luke 2:7). Public inns of the time were a type of caravansary where parties of travelers were lodged under a single roof. Often the travelers slept on the second floor, while their animals slept beneath them on the first floor (an inn was called a "habitation" in Jeremiah 41:17).[4] Patrons furnished their own bedding and food at these inns. Located along frequently traveled routes near water and pasture for their animals, caravansaries were built with high walls to surround arched alcoves that offered shelter but little if any privacy to travelers.

We know that Mary did not give birth in one of these caravansaries, because there was no room for her and Joseph "in the inns," as we have said, but the shelter in which Jesus

was born is not specified in the scriptures. Later Christian records assert that Mary gave birth to Jesus in a cave near Bethlehem.

Although the scriptures do not specifically state where Jesus was born, they do report that Mary "laid him in a manger" because of the lack of room in the inns (Luke 2:7). A manger (Greek, *phatnē*) most often refers to a trough, placed on the ground or created from a cavity in a rock, from which animals eat. The Greek translation of Isaiah uses the same word for "manger" in the following passage: "The ox knows his owner, and the ass his master's crib [manger]: but Israel does not know me, and the people has not regarded me" (Septuagint, or LXX, Isaiah 1:3). Christmas tradition adds animals to the scene, but the scriptures do not mention that Mary shared the place of Jesus' birth with sheep or donkeys. Nevertheless, we sense the humble surroundings in which young Mary gave birth to God's Only Begotten Son. President Brigham Young observed, "Others may have been born in as low a state as this, but it is hard to find anybody, among the civilized portions of mankind, that gets any lower."[5]

Without a word about a midwife or Joseph's role in attending the birth of Jesus, Luke focuses completely on Mary: "She brought forth her firstborn son, and wrapped him in swaddling clothes, and laid him in a manger" (Luke 2:7). We are drawn to Mary's efforts to care for her newborn child the best she could in the rude circumstances. Swaddling clothes were strips of cloth used to wrap around newborns. The baby was typically rubbed with oil before the strips of cloth were applied. Swaddling kept the baby warm, dry, and protected from skin infections.

Meanwhile, "in the same country," or in the open fields surrounding Bethlehem, shepherds were taking turns watching over their sheep through the watches of the night. In the Roman Empire, the night was divided into four watches from sundown to sunup.[6] We might not have anticipated that shepherds would be those selected by God as special witnesses. Sometimes caught grazing their flocks in other farmers' fields, shepherds were often viewed as dishonest and disloyal to the law of Moses.[7] These were not, however, typical shepherds. They must have had believing hearts and minds to have been chosen to receive the angel's visit. Elder Bruce R. McConkie even perceived the sheep as extraordinary when he surmised that they could have been "destined for sacrifice on the great altar in the Lord's House, in similitude of the eternal sacrifice of Him who that wondrous night lay in a stable, perhaps among sheep of lesser destiny."[8]

In the field near Bethlehem, however, those who were often considered to be the lowest among the low in the Jews' social order were invited to witness that the King of Kings had come. The scriptures do not specify why these men were chosen to be witnesses of such "good tidings of great joy," but their love of God and reverence for his word are clearly indicated by their actions (Luke 2:10). Of them, Elder James E. Talmage observed, "The trustful and unsophisticated keepers of sheep had not asked for sign or confirmation; their faith was in unison with the heavenly communication; nevertheless the angel had given them what he called a sign, to guide them in their search."⁹ When an angel from the Lord appeared to these shepherds in the silence of the night, at first they, like Mary, "were sore afraid" (Luke 2:9). Through direct revelation from God, the angel announced to them, "For unto you is born this day in the city of David a Saviour, which is Christ the Lord. And this shall be a sign unto you; ye shall find the babe wrapped in swaddling clothes, lying in a manger" (Luke 2:11–12).

A choir of heavenly angels echoed the announcement of the first angel with praise of God: "Glory to God in the highest, and on earth peace, good will toward men" (Luke 2:13–14). Whether the choir was made up of spirits who had once lived on earth or those waiting to be born, the emotion in their announcement would have been profound. They deeply understood and celebrated what few people on earth realized: "The hopes and fears of all the years are met in [the little town of Bethlehem] tonight."¹⁰

In reverent obedience to God, the shepherds left "with haste" to find Mary, Joseph, and the baby in the manger (Luke 2:16). Their immediate actions and clear direction also indicate their understanding that Bethlehem was "the city of David" (Luke 2:11). That very night they were privileged to behold their Savior soon after he came to earth in the flesh. Afterwards, the shepherds glorified and praised "God for all the things that they had heard and seen" (Luke 2:20). In return, Mary and Joseph received the added comfort and strength that came with additional witnesses to their wondrous miracle.

While shepherds "made known abroad the saying which was told them concerning this child," Mary pondered on "all these things" and kept "them in her heart" (Luke 2:17, 19). Reviewing *all* the miraculous support, protection, and direction God had already afforded her in her young life, she could discern his care and see that he had a plan for her and the child.

But how could she understand what lay before her? Rather than speak of sacred things that she did not fully comprehend or was unable to interpret correctly, she pondered what was happening to her and spoke nothing publicly of this miracle. Declaring her Son as the Anointed One of the Jews and the Savior of the world was not the errand that God had assigned to Mary. In addition to mothering the Son of God, her mission and testimony were evidenced through her diligent obedience to God's directions while allowing the Spirit to appropriately communicate to others the truth of his identity as the Son of God.

CHAPTER TEN

The Law of Moses and Childbirth

Four times in Luke 2 we are told that Mary and Joseph did things "according to the law of Moses" (v. 22), or the "law of the Lord" (vv. 23–24, 39), underscoring that they were humble followers of the law, including the ordinances pertaining to childbirth. Luke indicates that Mary and Joseph observed the rites of circumcision, purification, and redemption of the firstborn.

The law of circumcision. God established "a covenant of circumcision" (Acts 7:8) with Abraham and his male descendants when they were eight days old (Genesis 17:12) "that thou mayest know for ever that children are not accountable before me until they are eight years old" (JST, Genesis 17:11). In obedience to this law, Mary and Joseph took the eight-day-old Jesus to be circumcised and at the same time to officially give him the name Jesus, as the angel had instructed Mary "before he was conceived in the womb" (Luke

2:21) and as the angel had told Joseph before Mary went to live in his house (Matthew 1:21).

The law of purification for new mothers. Mary needed to be purified after giving birth (Luke 2:22–24), not she and Joseph or she and the baby. According to the law of Moses, birth, not conception, rendered a woman ritually unclean for seven days before a son was circumcised and thirty-three days afterwards, for a total of forty days (Leviticus 12:2–8). After giving birth to a daughter, the days a mother was "unclean" were doubled to eighty (Leviticus 12:5). No explanation for this difference is provided in scripture.

During her days of ritual impurity, a mother was not allowed to visit the temple or the sanctuary (Leviticus 12:4). "When the days of her purifying are fulfilled, for a son, or for a daughter," she was commanded to take to the "door of the tabernacle," or temple, a young lamb for a burnt offering and either "a young pigeon, or a turtledove, for a sin offering" (Leviticus 12:6). If a mother was "not able to bring a lamb, then she shall bring two turtle[dove]s, or two young pigeons; the one for the burnt offering, and the other for a sin offering: and the priest shall make an atonement for her, and she shall be clean" (Leviticus 12:8).

Luke does not record what Mary took to sacrifice for her purification, only that she fulfilled the law. For Herod's Temple, which was the temple in use during this time, the door is presumed to have been the gate on the west side of the Court of Women, which leads into the Court of the Israelites and the Court of Priests. This was the farthest point an Israelite woman could enter into the temple complex.

The law of redemption of the firstborn. In declaring Jesus the "firstborn son" of Mary (Luke 2:7), Luke was not implying that Mary would give birth to additional sons or that Jesus was the eldest, or first, of many. Rather, the Greek indicates simply that Mary had not given birth to a child before she gave birth to Jesus.[1] As the first to open the womb (Luke 2:23), Jesus had the blessings and responsibilities of the firstborn, according to Mosaic law (Exodus 13:1–2; Numbers 3:11–13; 18:15–16).

The birth of the firstborn also mandated special sacrifices under Jewish law. Originally, the firstborn was seen as belonging to God to serve him throughout his life; eventually, however, the tribe of Levi as a whole was assigned to bear this lifelong responsibility (Numbers 8:16). In exchange for "five shekels," the firstborn could be bought back, or redeemed, from the service of the Lord (Numbers 18:16). Parents of the firstborn were commanded to pay the price of redemption at the temple. Perhaps Luke did not mention payment for Jesus because he considered that Jesus also had Levite lineage and would therefore remain in God's service throughout his life.[2]

While at the temple to offer the sacrifices required by the law, Mary and Joseph were stopped by a man named Simeon, who was previously unknown to them. Luke does not call him a priest or give him any other position of special status to qualify him for the revelation he received at that moment. Simeon was qualified because he was "just

and devout, waiting for the consolation of Israel [the Messiah]: and the Holy Ghost was upon him" (Luke 2:25). That same Spirit had already promised Simeon he would not die "before he had seen the Lord's Christ" (Luke 2:26). On any given day, parents would be seen bringing their young children to the temple to offer the requisite devotions, but Simeon was led by the Spirit to the temple on the day Mary and Joseph brought the child Jesus there, and he immediately recognized him as the Messiah (Luke 2:27). Taking Mary's child into his arms, Simeon offered his own hymn, or canticle, called in Latin the Nunc Dimittis. This canticle contained two blessings—the first to God for preserving him until that moment (Luke 2:28–29) and the second for Mary and her child (Luke 2:34–35). Upon beholding the holy infant, Simeon praised God for "eyes [to see] thy salvation." He also bore witness that this Savior would be a light to the Gentiles as well as to Israel, literally to "all people" (Luke 2:30–31). Who else in Israel at this time could affirm that great truth? Understandably, Joseph and Mary "marvelled" at that which Simeon testified (Luke 2:33). Their reaction here echoes responses to other miraculous events, as recorded in Luke 1:21, 63 and 2:18.

In his blessing on the family, Simeon prophesied that Jesus was "set for the fall and rising again of many in Israel" (Luke 2:34). He would be seen as the cause for division among the Jews. The Greek verb translated here as "set" reflects imagery associated with building stones, suggesting that through the mission of Jesus Christ, Israel would experience destruction and yet rise again, like a building of stones, which is perhaps also a foreshadowing of resurrection.[3] Truly the Savior's mission would have expansive effects on the world, yet most would speak evil against him, Simeon forewarned, and would work to stop his efforts.

Simeon then turned to Mary. She too would undergo another challenging test of true discipleship. Simeon prophesied, "(A sword shall pierce through thy own soul also,) that the thoughts of many hearts may be revealed" (Luke 2:35). As presented in the King James Version of the Bible, this phrase about Mary's suffering is parenthetical, suggesting that the thoughts of those who reject Christ would be revealed, whereas her own suffering would be private.[4] Some have suggested that a sword figuratively pierced Mary's heart as a sword literally pierced her Son when he was crucified. Although it is John who records the scene of Mary at the crucifixion (John 19:25) and Luke discusses it not at all, Joseph Smith's translation of these words reinforces Simeon's meaning as figurative: "Yea, a spear shall pierce through him to the wounding of thine own soul also; that the thoughts of many hearts may be revealed" (JST, Luke 2:35). Others have suggested that Mary suffered each time Jesus was rejected. She could have felt the symbolic sword through her soul whenever she was maligned by people charging Jesus with being illegitimate or a fraud.

But Luke does not mention any of these meanings. Perhaps Mary experienced a broken heart, as we often do, while learning to accept and keep the word of God even when covenants supersede and transcend loyalty to our family. We cannot become perfect without suffering (JST, Hebrews 11:40). After all, a sword is double-edged and symbolically suggests the ability both to punish and to save. Later in his Gospel, Luke portrays Mary as one who exemplifies commitment to covenant, even amid suffering and heartache (Luke 8:21; Acts 1:14).

While the holy family was yet in the temple, an elderly woman named Anna came "in that instant" to them (Luke 2:38). Like Simeon she also recognized the Christ child and gave thanks to God for the blessing. Although the narrative does not specifically note how she received her revelation, she was called a "prophetess" (Luke 2:36). Like

Miriam, Deborah, and Huldah before her, Anna had the "spirit of prophecy," which is the testimony of Jesus (Revelation 19:10). Her title of prophetess indicates her openness to the Spirit for such revelation. She was also known as a descendant of the tribe of Asher, the eighth son of Jacob and the second son of Leah's handmaid, Zilpah. That an Asherite was living in Jerusalem at this time illustrates that the nation of the Jews was made up of representatives from potentially any of the twelve tribes, not only Judah, Levi, and Benjamin. A widow of some eighty-four years, Anna frequently fasted and prayed at the temple (Luke 2:37). This devout widow, one of perhaps a lower degree in the social order, was known and chosen by God to greet his Son and proclaim a reason to hope for all "that looked for redemption in Jerusalem" (Luke 2:38).

Mary worshiped God through her adherence to the sacrifices and other ordinances prescribed under the law of Moses. While she was doing what she and all other Jewish women were commanded to do, God blessed her. There at the temple, Mary encountered two additional witnesses, one male and one female, who bolstered her commitment to motherhood and served as a reminder of God's watchful eye. She would never be completely alone in the daunting assignment to rear the Son of God. We wonder how often she might have thought back on that day at the temple to remember that with God, nothing is impossible.

CHAPTER ELEVEN

The Escape to Egypt

Matthew's testimony alone reports that "wise men," or magi, visited the Holy Child and his mother. The identity, number, and geographical point of origin of these wise men are not given in scripture. We know only that they came "from the east" (Matthew 2:1). Various traditions portray them as coming from Persia or Babylon, where there was still a significant Jewish presence, but the earliest attested view claimed they came from Arabia.[1]

These magi did not coincidentally wander into Jerusalem soon after the Savior was born. They went purposefully, knowing of the Messiah's birth and having a desire to worship him. Only a few others in Judea had this knowledge—and that only through divine revelation. These men were no different. The wise men saw "his star in the east," where it rose, and knowing its significance through prophecy or perhaps by direct revelation, traveled to the land of the Jews "to worship him" (Matthew 2:2; JST, Matthew 3:2). Their recognition of the star's importance may indicate that these men were prophets or recipients of God's word, similar to Simeon, Anna, Zacharias, Elisabeth, Joseph, or the shepherds. Supporting the premise that they were prophets is the fact that as remarkable as this star appears to have been, there is no record of anyone else taking notice, let alone perceiving its stunning significance. Furthermore, the wise men were later warned by God through a dream (Matthew 2:12).

Because the wise men did not know precisely where to locate the Messiah upon their arrival in Jerusalem, they inquired of Herod—the nominal king of the Jews—for more information (Matthew 2:2–8). Going directly to Herod indicates their lack of awareness of Jerusalem's political situation and reveals Herod's pathological insecurity. Herod was "troubled" ("startled," in the Greek) upon learning that the Jews' rightful king had recently been born (Matthew 2:3). That was not what he had expected. History shows how paranoid he had become over his own sons who schemed to overthrow him. Now he would have to consider a greater threat from someone outside his own family.

With the help of the chief priests and scribes, Herod learned from Jewish scripture that the Christ would come out of Bethlehem (Micah 5:2), but he learned nothing more. Feigning an interest in adoring the young "King of the Jews," Herod sent the wise men "to Bethlehem, and said, Go and search diligently for the young child; and when ye have found him, bring me word again, that I may come and worship him also" (Matthew 2:2, 8).

THE ESCAPE TO EGYPT

In the testimonies of these wise men that the Messiah was born, we may see God's intent to alert all members of the Jewish population that the hope of their salvation was at hand. The working class could be told of his birth by the shepherds, the priestly and highly educated by the chief priests and scribes, the dutiful temple worshippers by Anna and Simeon, and the royal and aristocratic elite by Herod. "With this, we begin to see God's orchestrated scheme to reveal the presence of His Son among His people a full generation before His Son began ministering to others as Jesus of Nazareth."[2]

Only after the arrival of the wise men in Jerusalem does Matthew specifically indicate that the star actually guided them to the holy family, reporting that it "went before them, till it came and stood over where the young child was" (Matthew 2:9). Because real stars do not move to direct one's path in the way a flashlight does, Matthew may here be speaking of the star symbolically. In Jewish imagery, a star can symbolize an angel, as in Revelation 1:20, or being directed by angels.[3]

The scene of Mary and her Son that met the wise men was significantly different from that which the shepherds encountered. Whereas the shepherds found a newborn wrapped in swaddling clothes and lying in a manger, suggesting an area prepared for animals, the wise men found the family in a "*house*," and Jesus was described not as an infant but as a "*young child*" (Matthew 2:11; emphasis added; compare Luke 2:11–12). The temple in Jerusalem was still being built at this time. With Joseph's carpentry skills (Matthew 13:55), or perhaps more accurately translated, his "construction" skills, the family might have remained in the area because of the income a good carpenter or stonemason could earn by working on the temple.

There in Bethlehem, the wise men "opened their treasures," or treasure boxes filled with "gold, and frankincense, and myrrh," to give to the baby king, as was customary for foreign dignitaries when visiting royalty (Matthew 2:11). Because gold is linked with both frankincense and myrrh in this passage, it may refer to incense rather than to a metal. This theory is underscored when we consider that the Hebrew word for gold is reflected in the proto-Semitic root of the word, which in South Arabic indicated an aromatic substance instead of the precious metal. Some have therefore suggested that these gifts were coffers filled with incense, a luxury in first-century Palestine.[4]

Divine directives came to both Joseph and the wise men to warn them of Herod's design to "seek the young child to destroy him" (Matthew 2:13). In his rage and extreme paranoia, Herod ordered the death of "all the children . . . from two years old and under" in Bethlehem and its environs (Matthew 2:16). More specific in the Greek, the word *pais* used in this passage refers to male children in contrast to *teknon,* which means children generally, both male and female. Thus the text itself indicates that Herod's orders focused on young boys in Bethlehem. Concerning the number that would have been subject to the ruler's infamous edict, biblical scholar Raymond Brown noted, "Because of the high infant mortality rate, we are told that if the total population was one thousand [in Bethlehem], with an annual birthrate of thirty, the male children under two years of age would scarcely have numbered more than twenty."[5] Though this estimate of casualties is fewer than most of us have previously imagined, the slaughter of twenty infant boys is nonetheless heinous by any account.

In 7 B.C., not long before Herod carried out his massacre of the innocents, he ordered the death of his two favorite sons, Alexander and Aristobulous, who he believed were plotting to avenge his murder of their mother. Herod's reaction to the news of a Jewish Messiah is thus not surprising. Just five days before his own death, Herod executed his eldest son, Antipater.[6] Herod's infamous brutality toward family members reportedly inspired the emperor Augustus to quip, "It is better to be Herod's pig [*hys*] than his son [*huios*]."[7] In other words, while Jews would never slaughter pigs, which were unclean, Herod did not hesitate to slaughter his own sons.

Having been warned by dreams from God of Herod's intent to destroy young Jesus, the wise men "departed into their own country another way," rather than returning to report to Herod as they had agreed, and Joseph "took the young child and his mother by night, and departed into Egypt" (Matthew 2:12, 14). Because of its proximity, Egypt offered the family a sanctuary, as it had for many of God's people in times past.[8] God later sent an angel to Joseph in a dream to "take the young child and his mother, and go into the land of Israel: for they are dead which sought the young child's life" (Matthew 2:20; compare Exodus 4:19).

After Herod died in about 4 B.C., his son Archelaus ruled Judea in his stead. Although the Jews hoped for better treatment under the son, Archelaus proved even more brutal than his father.[9] Matthew indicates that the family's intent had been to return to the Bethlehem area in Judea to take up residence until Joseph was warned yet again through a vision. Changing course, the young family continued northward into eastern Galilee until they arrived again in Nazareth, where they would live throughout the Savior's childhood and into his adulthood (Matthew 2:22–23; JST, Matthew 2:19–25). Herod Antipas, another of Herod's sons, was given jurisdiction over Galilee and Perea after his father's death. Whereas Archelaus was soon removed from power in Judea and replaced by a series of Roman governors, Herod Antipas was still in power when Jesus began his ministry and remained the tetrarch of these areas during the Savior's ministry, trials, and death.

Although little about Mary's life during the first years after she gave birth to Jesus is recounted in scripture, we wonder if she might have been surprised at some events involving her son. We wonder how often the family changed residences, including the temporary move to a foreign land, which naturally disrupted the domestic order. In the years after Jesus' birth, Mary and Joseph apparently had other children, beginning with a son they named James (Matthew 13:55; Mark 6:3). Because Mary's later children are not mentioned in the scriptural narrative until the Savior's ministry, we do not know the age difference between Jesus and James. Considering reactions of modern-day mothers to children of differing sensitivities, we might imagine that Mary understood the joys and immense challenges associated with mothering multiple children who differed from each other.

CHAPTER TWELVE

Mothering the Child Jesus

The scriptural record is virtually silent about Mary and her family during the next several years. Luke simply summarizes these years with a description of the young Jesus: "And the child grew, and waxed strong in spirit, filled with wisdom: and the grace of God was upon him" (Luke 2:40). Watching her child grow from a helpless infant into a spiritually strong and exceptionally wise young man must have given Mary daily cause to marvel. She would have watched his physical growth much as other parents do, considering it occurred at a normal pace. But his spiritual and intellectual growth must have been astounding, quickly exceeding what she could teach him. The Joseph Smith Translation indicates that "he spake not as other men, neither could he be taught" (JST, Matthew 3:25). How often Mary must have felt inadequate, humbled, and also profoundly blessed to be this gifted child's mother. No doubt her own commitment to diligence in God's service was enhanced through observations of her completely and strikingly diligent Son.

President Joseph Fielding Smith suggested the various ways young Jesus could have been tutored during his primary years. "Evidently, before he was 12 years old," President Smith taught, "[Jesus] had learned a great deal about his Father's business. This knowledge could come to him by revelation, by visitation of angels, or in some other way. But his knowledge, so far as this life was concerned, had to come line upon line and precept upon precept."[1]

One specific incident is recorded in scripture of the Savior's later childhood. Joseph and Mary had travelled to Jerusalem for the feast of the Passover, as was their custom. Whether they took Jesus with them the previous years is not known, but in the year when Jesus was twelve years old, the Jewish year of manhood, he did accompany them (Luke 2:41–42).

Under the law of Moses, adult males were specifically required to appear at the sanctuary three times a year; the law names as the three holy weeks of the year Passover, or the feast of unleavened bread; Pentecost, or the feast of weeks; and Succoth, or the feast of tabernacles (Deuteronomy 16:16; Exodus 34:23). Many Jews lived far from Jerusalem and even from Palestine in the early first century, so it is likely that a great number would have made the pilgrimage only once a year or perhaps even once in a lifetime. The law does not mention any requirement for women and children in this regard, and the Mishnah notably exempts women from such travel.² That Mary made the trek annually underscores her spiritual nature and active faith (Luke 2:41).

After completing the duties associated with the feast, Mary and Joseph began making their way back north to Nazareth in the company of "their kinsfolk and acquaintance," people most likely also from the same area (Luke 2:44). Supposing that the twelve-year-old Jesus was somewhere in the travelling party, "Joseph and his mother" did not notice until the end of the first day of travel that he had remained in Jerusalem. Returning the approximately twenty miles the next day, they searched the city on the third day and finally found him at the temple "after three days" (Luke 2:43, 46). They came upon him "sitting in the midst of the doctors [teachers], and they were hearing him, and asking him questions" (JST, Luke 2:46).

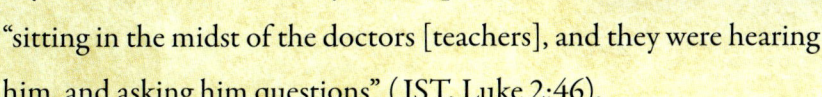

The Jewish teachers in the temple reacted to the boy's wisdom with the same awe and wonder as had those who heard the shepherds' report (Luke 2:18) and as Mary and Joseph had responded to Simeon's canticle (Luke 2:33). According to Luke, the scene caused Mary and Joseph again to be "amazed"

(Luke 2:48). Because Mary and Joseph had received revelations about Jesus' divine identity and throughout his childhood, they had observed his remarkable spiritual growth, to which they alone had been privy, it may seem surprising at first that Mary and Joseph could be awed by the scene at the temple.

But the scene seems to have put in a new light the rapidity with which Jesus learned and the depth of wisdom he had achieved, all while looking like a normal boy of twelve.

The Prophet Joseph Smith taught that Jesus progressed intellectually and spiritually more dramatically than he did physically, as

shown by his superior understanding before the Jewish intellectuals at the temple that day: "When still a boy, He had all the intelligence necessary to enable Him to rule and govern the kingdom of the Jews, and could reason with the wisest and most profound doctors of law and divinity, and make their theories and practice to appear like folly compared with the wisdom He possessed; but He was a boy only, and lacked physical strength even to defend His own person; and was subject to cold, to hunger, and to death."[3] Most likely Mary experienced surprise and increased awe in her daily interactions with young Jesus.

At the temple in Jerusalem, Mary's first words rang with what seems to be a tone of reproach but probably more deeply reflected the fear and anguish that had built inside her over the past two days: "Son, why hast thou thus dealt with us? behold, thy father and I have sought thee sorrowing" (Luke 2:48). Her words are understandable to parents who have felt the terror of not knowing where their child is. Similarly, Jesus' response should be seen not as criticism for their anguish and worry but as sadness that they knew him so little. They should have guessed immediately that he would be at his Father's house. "How is it that ye sought me?" he asked them. "[Did ye not know] that I must be about my Father's business?" (Luke 2:49). But Mary and Joseph did not comprehend the full import of what this twelve-year-old boy was saying (Luke 2:50). Again, the contrast in understanding between Jesus and all others, including Mary, his mother, is quite marked.

Throughout this exchange at the temple and the many teachings in the years that followed, Jesus shows us the power and wisdom that come from giving our relationship with the Father first priority. Because Jesus' commitment to his Father in Heaven transcended mortal family ties, he was able to bless Mary and all of humankind. Nothing—not even his love for his mother—could distract him from his foreordained mission. He was not yet prepared, however, to commence his official ministry. Apparently that preparation included additional lessons to be learned within the family, lessons presented back at home in Nazareth.

Leaving the temple, Jesus returned to Nazareth with Mary and Joseph "and was subject unto them" (Luke 2:51). Although he already knew by this young age that he was God's Son and that he excelled in wisdom over everyone around him, he meekly obeyed his mortal parents. The unavoidable tie between willing obedience and wisdom is established again. Might this exchange at the temple and Jesus' subsequent submission to Mary have intensified both her confusion and her reverence for her Son when they returned to Nazareth? As Jesus continued to increase "in wisdom and stature, and in favour with God and man," his mother was the one most likely to notice (Luke 2:52). Wisely, she "kept all these sayings in her heart" (Luke 2:51). Instinctively, she seemed to recognize that the answers to her questions would not come by broadcasting her observations to those around her or by complaining of her unique challenges to her neighbors. Instead, she pondered what she had been given and prepared herself to gain additional insights that would eventually lead her to understanding. Like her Son, she was gaining that understanding line upon line, grace by grace, albeit at a much slower pace than she might have wished.

And he went down with them, and came to Nazareth, and was subject unto them: *but his mother kept all these sayings in her heart*

CHAPTER THIRTEEN

During the Savior's Mortal Ministry

Little is communicated in the scriptures about Mary's life and character once the Savior began his ministry. The implication of the four Gospels is that she was more often at home with her family, as was customary for Jewish women of that day, than always accompanying Jesus in his travels. Jesus was known by his neighbors in Nazareth simply as "the carpenter's son" (Matthew 13:55), suggesting perhaps the ordinariness of Jesus' birth and childhood. The villagers were apparently unaware of his royal lineage, his miraculous escape from Herod's heinous edict in Judea, or his being visited by mysterious magi from the East. All of this again indicates the maturity, wisdom, and restraint exercised by Mary throughout her Son's mortal life.

An incident in Nazareth after Jesus had become known for his miracles in other parts of Galilee further illustrates Mary's success in giving Jesus a normal childhood. Jesus went to the synagogue on the Sabbath day "as his custom was" and was invited to participate in the weekly Torah reading. After reading aloud a passage from Isaiah that speaks messianically and in the first person, Jesus offered the following commentary: "This day is this scripture fulfilled in your ears" (Luke 4:21).

The townspeople of Nazareth, Mary's neighbors and friends, who would have watched Jesus grow up before their eyes, "wondered at the gracious words which proceeded out of his mouth. And they said, Is not this Joseph's son?" (Luke 4:22). In Mark's account of this event, the people in the synagogue asked, "Is not this the carpenter, the son of Mary, the brother of James, and Joses, and of Juda, and Simon? And are not his sisters here with us?" (Mark 6:3). They spoke of Mary's family with familiarity: "Is not this Jesus, the son of Joseph, whose father and mother we know?" (John 6:42). To these Galileans, Jesus was merely the son of people they knew well, so how could he be the powerful and wise figure he implied himself to be through the witness of the Spirit?

Even their expectations of seeing the kind of healing Jesus had performed in nearby Capernaum, however, did not prepare them for the spiritual outpouring that accompanied his teaching in their synagogue. They must have mused, "This certainly could not be the one whom the Spirit identified as the Anointed One," for there was nothing unusual about Jesus' childhood. "This is Joseph's son, not God's Son," they apparently thought. When Jesus pointed out their stubbornness about accepting the truth set before them, adding examples from the Old Testament of Gentiles who responded more readily to the

Spirit than they were responding, the villagers became angry enough to try to kill him (Luke 4:24–30). The reaction of the villagers of Nazareth to Jesus during his ministry indirectly points to Mary's having so well deflected attention away from the divinity of her Son that he was allowed to grow up without unnecessary opposition.

We see Mary again early in Jesus' ministry when they both attended a wedding feast at Cana, a Galilean village less than ten miles north of Nazareth. During the wedding feast, probably the night the groom came to take his bride to his home, the host of the feast had somehow run out of wine, a social embarrassment (John 2:1–3). Upon discovering this oversight, Mary instinctively turned to her Son, fully believing that he could somehow resolve the problem. By this time, she already had complete confidence and faith in his abilities, knowing what Peter would later discover: There was no one else to go to for help (John 6:68). Recognizing her faith in him, Jesus responded to her request for help not only by miraculously producing more wine but by producing better wine than had been previously served, much to the amazement of the guest of honor.

To his mother alone, however, Jesus offered the significant comment, "Mine hour is not yet come" (John 2:4), foreshadowing Gethsemane (John 13:1; 17:1; Mark 14:41).

Mine hour is not yet come

The miracle at Cana was not his hour, but it could help Mary understand that hour when it came. When it did, Jesus, the "true vine" (John 15:1, 5), went into Gethsemane, the garden of "the oil press," and shed his blood (*Gethsemane* means "oil press" in Aramaic). Then and there, Jesus gave humankind the wine of the Atonement, the very best wine, of which the Saints symbolically drink when they partake of the sacrament (Luke 22:19–20, 44).

> *There was no other good enough*
>
> *To pay the price of sin.*
>
> *He only could unlock the gate*
>
> *Of heav'n and let us in.*[1]

The Son of Mary was the *only* one whose atoning blood could satisfy the demands of justice. Furthermore, his gift of wine for the wedding guests anticipated the great gift of salvation he would give to all mankind.

At the wedding feast, Jesus addressed his mother as "Woman" (John 2:4). Although not impolite or disrespectful in any way at the time, this was perhaps an unusual manner for a Jewish son to address his mother. Perhaps by calling his mother "Woman," he directs us to remember scripture's first reference to the Savior's mother. In the Eden narrative, our Redeemer was described simply as the "seed" of "the woman" (Genesis 3:15). Mary was *the* one and only woman to give birth to a son who had no mortal father: Jesus was the seed of Adam's female descendant, the woman, and not of her husband.

By calling his mother "Woman," Jesus may also have reminded Mary that he put a higher priority on his Father's work than on his mortal family, as discussed earlier. Was he telling her that she could not assume he would continue to be at her beck and call simply because she was his mother? Through the Atonement, Mary, like the rest of humankind, had to become *his* daughter (Mosiah 5:7).

Jesus would later teach that sincerely loving God should take a higher priority in our hearts than love for others, including family (Matthew 22:36–40; 10:37). The commandment not to have any other gods come ahead of the Lord God preceded the command to honor father and mother (Exodus 20:2, 12). Our ability to love others, including family members, will always be enhanced and informed when God comes first in our lives.

At the same time, the verbal exchange during the wedding feast at Cana shows the Savior's sensitivity to his mother. Unlike so many of his later miracles, when Jesus turned water to wine in Cana, the phenomenon was not accompanied with the exclamations of astounded bystanders. Perhaps the perception of the miracle was for his mother alone, an affirmation of her strength and support through years of pondering so many things in her heart. When the celebration concluded, Jesus and his disciples accompanied Mary and his brothers to Capernaum for a few days before departing from his family to continue his ministry (John 2:12).

Because Joseph is not present in any scene after his discovery of the boy Jesus at the temple in Luke 2:41–51, most scholars assume that Mary was widowed before the Savior's ministry began. James, Jesus' younger half-brother and author of the epistle, defined "pure religion and undefiled before God and the Father" as "to visit the fatherless and widows in their affliction" (James 1:27). If indeed Joseph did die early in the Savior's and James's lives, the widowed Mary and her fatherless children may have first experienced pure religion through selfless acts of kindness they received.

The suggestion that Mary likely was not often alone with Jesus does not mean she independently chose to remain at home and away from him. In the absence of the father in Jewish homes, the eldest son typically ruled the family. Because Jesus was away from home more often than not, that responsibility would likely fall on the next oldest, or James. If James did not agree with Jesus' message and mission and Jesus was absent, thus leaving James in charge, Mary would not have had the freedom to support Jesus as she desired.

Hints about Jesus' half-brothers in the scriptures imply their resistance to the Savior's work during his mortality. During the Savior's ministry, James and his younger brothers not only were nonbelievers in Jesus' divinity but seem to have been embarrassed by his behavior and notoriety. For example, Mark reports that Jesus observed, "A prophet is not without honour, but . . . in his own house" (Mark 6:4). The same Gospel says that his family (in Greek, "those near to him or those of his own," which scholars conclude means "his family," rather than the KJV translation "his friends") said Jesus was "beside himself," or crazy (Mark 3:21).[2] Moreover, after Jews in Galilee rejected Jesus because of his Bread of Life sermon and Jews in Jerusalem sought his life because of miracles and condemnatory teachings, Jesus' brothers encouraged him to depart from them in Galilee and return to Jerusalem, "for neither did his brethren believe in him" (John 7:5). Despite Mary's own beliefs and religious desires, her actions would have been restricted by the family's presiding male. At the very least, Mary would have known the heartache that plagues a part-member family or a parent of unbelieving children.

At least once, Mary went with the brothers of Jesus to where Jesus was teaching (Mark 3:31; see also Luke 8:19). Jewish scribes from Jerusalem had journeyed to Galilee to stir up opposition against him (Mark 3:22–30). In the middle of Jesus' teachings, the crowd alerted him to his family's presence. Jesus asked, "Who is my mother, or my brethren?" Then, gesturing to the multitude, he added, "Behold my mother and my brethren! For whosoever shall do the will of God, the same is my brother, and my sister, and mother" (Mark 3:35; see also Luke 8:19–21).

From the context, it seems Jesus was teaching the people about discipleship when his mother and brothers approached. With their arrival and the attention brought to

DURING THE SAVIOR'S MORTAL MINISTRY

them by someone in the crowd—"Behold thy mother and thy brethren without seek for thee" (Mark 3:32)—he found an opportunity to illustrate the principle that those who follow his teachings are his family. Blood relationship is not a substitute for discipleship. In a similar exchange with a woman from the crowd who expressed her appreciation for him by blessing his mother, or "the womb that bare thee, and the paps which thou hast sucked," Jesus responded, "Yea rather, blessed are they that hear the word of God, and keep it" (Luke 11:27–28).

Although James and his younger brothers did not at this time "believe on [Jesus]" (John 7:5), nowhere does scripture indicate that Mary was a nonbeliever. Faith includes remaining steadfastly loyal to the Savior, and Mary possessed such faith, from her initial call by Gabriel to be the mother of God's Son to the cross and through all the heartache in between. The Savior's inclusion of the multitude with his family did not diminish his love for his mother or his reverence for motherhood. Rather, his teachings on these topics underscore that it is not the act of giving birth—even to the Son of God—that qualifies a person to receive God's greatest blessings. The requisite qualification is sacrifice, which every person is capable of making. Anyone who hears, receives, and willingly follows his gospel is blessed. Mary's blessed state grew out of her reverence for God's word, not because she gave birth to his Son.

One other incident hints that ugly rumors may have cast a shadow over Mary during her Son's life. As some of the Jewish leaders were seeking to find fault with him, Jesus spoke of Abraham's children as those who "do the works of Abraham" (John 8:39). According to Jesus, because these Jewish leaders sought to kill him, they could be considered not as Abraham's children but rather as children of the devil, who sanctions such heinous deeds. To this offense the Jewish leaders spat back at Jesus, "*We* be not born of fornication," suggesting that Jesus was shamefully born (John 8:41; emphasis added). They appear to have been calling Jesus illegitimate, thereby implying that his mother was guilty of fornication and thus he could be disqualified as a legitimate religious authority

(Deuteronomy 23:2). Elder McConkie saw in the Jews' remark, "We be not born of fornication" not as a reference to inherited mortal lineage but as a reference to spiritual lineage. He explained the passage by paraphrasing what they said as, "The devil is not our father; we are not spiritually illegitimate; we are the children of Abraham and have the true religion, and hence God is our Father."[3]

No evidence survives to suggest how Mary responded to embarrassment created by false conclusions about her or her firstborn son. Nor are we told of her reactions to divisions among her own family. She may have replied in the same way she did after the annunciation—pondering and praying for understanding. Most important, the scripture narrative indicates that she did not have an easy life and that answers to her prayers did not come quickly. Mary knew the reality of an imperfect world, made more intense by her early encounter with the divine.

CHAPTER FOURTEEN

Jesus' Suffering and Death

Other than during the wedding feast in Cana (John 2:1–10), John speaks of Mary only one other time—at the scene of the crucifixion, where she was standing near the cross (John 19:25). Here again John refers to Mary not by name but by her role as Jesus' mother, perhaps emphasizing Jesus' mortality by reminding us of his mortal mother (John 19:26). In John's Gospel, the reality of Jesus' divinity cannot be hidden. He is presented as "the Word" and "the Lamb of God" who came from the presence of God and created "all things" (John 1:1, 36, 3). He is the great "I Am" (the Jehovah of the Old Testament), "the Light of the World," and "the Bread of Life" (John 8:58; 8:12; 6:35). At the same time, he was "made flesh," the son of a woman whose geographical origins and family connections were known (John 1:14).

Both the human and divine attributes were present in Jesus as he hung on the cross and suffered "temptations, and pain of body, hunger, thirst, and fatigue, even more than man can suffer" (Mosiah 3:7). In referring to Mary as the mother of Jesus, John reminds us that the Savior's pains were human and real, his agony immense. Because Jesus is also the Only Begotten of the Father, he could honestly say, "No man taketh it [my life] from me, but I lay it down of myself. I have power to lay it down, and I have power to take it again. This commandment have I received of my Father" (John 10:18).

None of Mary's words are recorded in John's depiction of the crucifixion; her only action is standing by the cross. To see Mary standing, however, does not suggest that she was passively waiting or even was paralyzed with grief. Because thinking, reflecting, and analyzing are valuable attributes that are often lacking in eras of constant distraction and immediate gratification, we may fail to consider that with her meditative qualities, Mary could learn while the world stirred around her. Standing by Jesus in what others perceived as a shameful predicament, Mary communicated that her fear of God was greater than her fear of man. Whatever accusation a bystander could fling at her, Mary's stoic stance beside her Son communicates that unlike others of his disciples, she would not deny her association with Jesus. More than remaining loyal to a son, Mary was a stalwart disciple of her redeemer.

Other women were with Mary at the cross, but John offers us only the briefest description of them. In fact, the passage does not make it clear whether there were three women or four near the cross. "Now there stood by the cross of Jesus his mother, and his mother's sister, Mary the wife of Cleophas, and Mary Magdalene" (John 19:25). This is the only mention of Mary's sister, who, due to the ambiguity in the text, may also have been named Mary. Because two sisters are unlikely to have shared the same given name, we will consider that four women were at the cross, rather than three. Concluding, then, that Mary's sister is unnamed, Mary the wife of Cleophas must be a different woman. Luke speaks of a disciple named Cleopas (Luke 24:18), but this passage in John records the only mention of the wife of Cleophas. Finally, John tells us that Mary Magdalene stood near the mother of Jesus at the cross. Luke introduces us to Mary Magdalene as an early disciple of Christ (Luke 8:2), but this is the first time John includes her in his testimony. The implication is that these women, including the mother of Jesus, were devoted followers of the Savior and probably all from Galilee, if we consider parallel accounts in the synoptic Gospels (Matthew 27:55–56; Mark 15:40–41).

In this poignant scene, filled with overwhelming pain, grief, and foreboding loneliness, it was Jesus who spoke first. And just as he did in Cana, according to John 2:4, Jesus addressed his mother as "Woman." "When Jesus therefore saw his mother, and the disciple standing by, whom he loved, he saith unto his mother, Woman, behold thy son! Then saith he to the disciple, Behold thy mother! And from that hour that disciple took her unto his own home" (John 19:26–27). Even in his excruciating pain, Jesus was expressing compassion for individuals and teaching the importance of service. The assumption that arises when he assigned the care of his mother to a beloved disciple, presumably the author of the Gospel of John, is that James and the other biological half-brothers of Jesus were not yet Christians. Many interpret from this scene the Savior's emotional, passion-filled expression of love for his mother in his final moments of mortality. Yet Jesus did not give a charge only to the beloved disciple; Mary also received a commission. He was not merely divesting himself of his family obligations as the eldest son; he was assigning Mary another son to mother in his place: "Inasmuch as ye have [shown compassion to one another], ye have done it unto me" (Matthew 25:40).

Others see the scene through a more symbolic lens, positing that Mary represents the Church, as does the woman in Revelation 12:1–6, and that John represents all the disciples who love the Lord, portrayed in Revelation 12:7–11 as those who fought against the dragon. On the other hand, John may have been focusing less on Mary and the beloved disciple and more on the conclusion of Jesus' mortal mission. In the Savior's final moments in mortality, we see his mother and other disciples acutely aware of their need for him. He alone performed the atoning sacrifice, died, and after three days rose again, to depart eventually in glory (Acts 1:9–11).

God's offer of salvation to the world came not only *through* Mary but also *for* her. Mary and the other disciples remained on earth as witnesses of their redeemer. They remind us that no family connection or ecclesiastical position of authority supersedes the dependence we all have on Jesus Christ for hope and salvation.

CHAPTER FIFTEEN

After the Resurrection

Mary's commitment to God was evident from the time of Gabriel's annunciation that she was "highly favoured" of God (Luke 1:28). She showed remarkable faith in accepting her mission to become the mother of the Son of God. More unexpected occurrences caused her to ponder in her heart what was happening around her and what the divine truths she had been told really meant. She kept all these things in her heart, rather than spread them abroad, allowing herself gradually to gain a greater witness and understanding of her Son's unique mission.

Luke gives us our final glimpse of Mary. After the Savior's forty-day, postresurrection ministry, she joined her surviving children and other disciples (numbering 120 in all) to pray and worship together (Acts 1:14). Unexpectedly, we read that the brothers of Jesus were at this time numbered with the believers. They must have experienced a mighty change of heart in the intervening weeks since Jesus had died. The apostle Paul gives one hint to explain this conversion, observing that the resurrected Lord appeared to his half-brother James, presumably during the forty-day ministry (1 Corinthians 15:7). James eventually became a key Christian leader in Jerusalem after the death of James, brother of John (Acts 15:13–20; 21:17–19); he and another half-brother, Jude/Judas, each wrote an epistle that became part of the New Testament. The record is silent concerning Mary's reaction to this newfound religious harmony in her family, but any believing parent who has witnessed a doubting child repent and embrace the gospel could empathize with Mary as she worshipped with her family.

Mary would likely not yet have been fifty years old at the time of Jesus' resurrection, but the scriptures do not tell us anything about her health or her later years. Naturally, legends abound, but reliable information about her ends with the passage in Acts 1:14. From Luke's portrait of her with the Christians after the Resurrection, Mary's prayer, "Behold the handmaid of the Lord; be it unto me according to thy word" (Luke 1:38), was answered, and she remained loyal to God's word throughout her life.

Scripture most often employs Mary to further portray Jesus Christ. As she proclaimed in the Magnificat, "My soul doth magnify the Lord" (Luke 1:46). Through her experiences, Mary invites us to see our Savior more clearly. Her example as a mother and as a disciple heightens our perspective as we grow in awe of God's almighty goodness and power in our daily walk with each other.

Notes

Chapter One
Mary, the Mother of Jesus

1. Joseph A. Fitzmyer, *The Gospel According to Luke I–IX,* Anchor Bible series (New York: Doubleday, 1982), 344.

2. Irenaeus, *Against Heresies*, 3.22.4, in *Ante-Nicene Fathers: The Writings of the Fathers Down to A.D. 325*, ed. Alexander Roberts, James Donaldson, and A. Cleveland Coxe, 10 vols. (Peabody, Mass.: Hendrickson, 1999), 1:455.

3. Gail Corrington Streete, "Women as Sources of Redemption and Knowledge in Early Christian Traditions," in *Women and Christian Origins*, ed. Ross Shepard Kraemer and Mary Rose D'Angelo (New York: Oxford University Press, 1999), 348.

4. Bruce R. McConkie, *The Mortal Messiah: From Bethlehem to Calvary*, 4 vols. (Salt Lake City: Deseret Book, 1981), 1:326–27.

Chapter Two
Prophecies concerning Mary

1. Daniel C. Peterson, Matthew Roper, and William J. Hamblin, "On Alma 7:10 and the Birthplace of Jesus Christ," available at http://maxwellinstitute.byu.edu. See also John A. Tvedtnes, "Cities and

Notes

Lands in the Book of Mormon," *Journal of Book of Mormon Studies* 4, no. 2 (1995): 147–50; available at http://maxwellinstitute.byu.edu.

Chapter Three
Childhood of Jewish Girls

1. Philo, Special Laws, 3.31, *The Works of Philo: Complete and Unabridged*, trans. C. D. Yonge (Peabody, Mass.: Hendrickson, 1993), 611.
2. Joachim Jeremias, *Jerusalem in the Time of Jesus* (Philadelphia: Fortress Press, 1969), 362–63.
3. Lynn H. Cohick, *Women in the World of the Earliest Christians: Illuminating Ancient Ways of Life* (Grand Rapids, Mich.: Baker, 2009), 232.
4. "Dress and Ornamentation," in *Anchor Bible Dictionary*, ed. David Noel Freedman, 6 vols. (New York: Doubleday, 1992), 2:237. See also Joseph and Aseneth, 14.12–17, in *The Old Testament Pseudepigrapha*, ed. James H. Charlesworth, trans. C. Burchard, 2 vols. (Garden City, N.Y.: Doubleday, 1985), 2:225. Although Joseph and Aseneth lived around the seventeenth century B.C., this document was a Jewish work of the first century B.C. to the second century A.D. It is therefore descriptive of customs of the New Testament era.

Chapter Four
Jewish Marriage Customs

1. Ketuboth, 3.1.8, in *The Mishnah*, trans. Herbert Danby (Oxford: Oxford University Press, 1992), 249. A girl was considered to have reached puberty at the age of twelve years and a day. Kiddushin, 1.2, in *Mishnah*, 321.
2. Pirke Aboth, 5.21, in *Mishnah*, 458.
3. Pesahim, 3.7, in *Mishnah*, 139.
4. Ketuboth, 4.4–5, in *Mishnah*, 250.
5. Lynn H. Cohick, *Women in the World of the Earliest Christians: Illuminating Ancient Ways of Life* (Grand Rapids, Mich.: Baker, 2009), 61.
6. Joachim Jeremias, *Jerusalem in the Time of Jesus* (Philadelphia: Fortress Press, 1969), 368.

NOTES

Chapter Five
The Annunciation in Nazareth

1. "Nazareth," in *Anchor Bible Dictionary,* ed. David Noel Freedman, 6 vols. (New York: Doubleday, 1992), 4:1050.

2. S. Kent Brown, *Mary and Elisabeth: Noble Daughters of God* (American Fork, Utah: Covenant Communications, 2002), 37; Eric D. Huntsman, *Good Tidings of Great Joy: An Advent Celebration of the Savior's Birth* (Salt Lake City: Deseret Book, 2011), 48.

3. Joseph Smith, *Teachings of the Prophet Joseph Smith,* sel. Joseph Fielding Smith (Salt Lake City: Deseret Book, 1976), 157.

4. Beverly R. Gaventa, *Mary: Glimpses of the Mother of Jesus* (Columbia: University of South Carolina Press, 1995), 53.

5. James E. Talmage, *Jesus the Christ,* Classics in Mormon Literature ed. (Salt Lake City: Deseret Book, 1983), 77.

6. Raymond E. Brown, *The Birth of the Messiah: A Commentary on the Infancy Narratives in Matthew and Luke* (New York: Doubleday, 1977), 344.

Chapter Six
Joseph

1. S. Kent Brown, *Mary and Elisabeth: Noble Daughters of God* (American Fork, Utah: Covenant Communications, 2002), 48.

2. Raymond E. Brown, *The Birth of the Messiah: A Commentary on the Infancy Narratives in Matthew and Luke* (New York: Doubleday, 1977), 128.

Chapter Seven
Mary's Lineage

1. James E. Talmage, *Jesus the Christ,* Classics in Mormon Literature ed. (Salt Lake City: Deseret Book, 1983), 75–76.

Notes

2. Lynn H. Cohick, *Women in the World of the Earliest Christians: Illuminating Ancient Ways of Life* (Grand Rapids, Mich.: Baker, 2009), 154.

Chapter Eight
Mary's Visit to Elisabeth

1. S. Kent Brown, *Mary and Elisabeth: Noble Daughters of God* (American Fork, Utah: Covenant Communications, 2002), 39.
2. "O Little Town of Bethlehem," *Hymns of The Church of Jesus Christ of Latter-day Saints* (Salt Lake City: The Church of Jesus Christ of Latter-day Saints, 1985), no. 208.
3. Raymond E. Brown, *The Birth of the Messiah: A Commentary on the Infancy Narratives in Matthew and Luke* (New York: Doubleday, 1977), 314.
4. Brown, *Birth of the Messiah*, 333.
5. Brown, *Birth of the Messiah*, 334–35, 340–41.
6. Brown, *Birth of the Messiah*, 337.
7. Brown, *Birth of the Messiah*, 338.

Chapter Nine
Jesus' Birth in Bethlehem

1. Lincoln H. Blumell and Thomas A. Wayment, "When Was Jesus Born?" unpublished manuscript.
2. Reuben J. Swanson, ed., *New Testament Greek Manuscripts: Luke* (Sheffield, England: Sheffield Academic Press, 1995), 30.
3. Beverly R. Gaventa, *Mary: Glimpses of the Mother of Jesus* (Columbia: University of South Carolina Press, 1995), 60.
4. "Inn," in William Smith, *The New Smith's Bible Dictionary*, ed. Reuel G. Lemmons (New York: Doubleday, 1966), 157. See also Alfred Edersheim, *The Life and Times of Jesus the Messiah* (Peabody, Mass.: Hendrickson, 1993), 130.
5. Brigham Young, in *Journal of Discourses,* 26 vols. (Liverpool: F. D. Richards and Sons, 1855–86), 3:366.

NOTES

6. See LDS Bible Dictionary, "Watches," 788.
7. Raymond E. Brown, *The Birth of the Messiah: A Commentary on the Infancy Narratives in Matthew and Luke* (New York: Doubleday, 1977), 420.
8. Bruce R. McConkie, *The Mortal Messiah: From Bethlehem to Calvary*, 4 vols. (Salt Lake City: Deseret Book, 1981), 1:347.
9. James E. Talmage, *Jesus the Christ*, Classics in Mormon Literature ed. (Salt Lake City: Deseret Book, 1983), 89.
10. "O Little Town of Bethlehem," *Hymns of The Church of Jesus Christ of Latter-day Saints* (Salt Lake City: The Church of Jesus Christ of Latter-day Saints, 1985), no. 208.

Chapter Ten
The Law of Moses and Childbirth

1. Joseph A. Fitzmyer, *The Gospel According to Luke I-IX*, Anchor Bible series (New York: Doubleday, 1982), 407.
2. *Mary in the New Testament*, ed. Raymond E. Brown, Karl P. Donfried, Joseph A. Fitzmyer, and John Reumann (Philadephia: Fortress Press, 1978), 153–54.
3. Raymond E. Brown, *The Birth of the Messiah: A Commentary on the Infancy Narratives in Matthew and Luke* (New York: Doubleday, 1977), 460–66.
4. Brown et. al., *Mary in the New Testament*, 155–56.

Chapter Eleven
The Escape to Egypt

1. See Justin Martyr, *Dialogue with Trypho*, chap. 78, and Tertullian, *Against Marcion,* 3.13, in *Ante-Nicene Fathers: The Writings of the Fathers Down to A.D. 325,* ed. Alexander Roberts, James Donaldson, and A. Cleveland Coxe, 10 vols. (Peabody, Mass.: Hendrickson, 1999), 3:237, 332.
2. S. Kent Brown, *Mary and Elisabeth: Noble Daughters of God* (American Fork, Utah: Covenant Communications, 2002), 60.

NOTES

3. *Joseph and Aseneth,* 14.1–3, in *The Old Testament Pseudepigrapha,* ed. James H. Charlesworth, trans. C. Burchard, 2 vols. (Garden City, N.Y.: Doubleday, 1985), 2:224.

4. Raymond E. Brown, *The Birth of the Messiah: A Commentary on the Infancy Narratives in Matthew and Luke* (New York: Doubleday, 1977), 176.

5. Brown, *Birth of the Messiah,* 204.

6. Flavius Josephus, *Antiquities of the Jews,* 16.1–11; 17.8.1, in *The Works of Josephus, Complete and Unabridged,* trans. William Whiston (Peabody, Mass.: Hendrickson, 1996), 426–50, 464.

7. Brown, *Birth of the Messiah,* 226.

8. Eric D. Huntsman, *Good Tidings of Great Joy: An Advent Celebration of the Savior's Birth* (Salt Lake City: Deseret Book, 2011), 109.

9. Josephus, *Antiquities of the Jews,* 17.11.2, in *Works of Josephus,* 472.

Chapter Twelve
Mothering the Child Jesus

1. Joseph Fielding Smith, *Doctrines of Salvation,* comp. Bruce R. McConkie, 3 vols. (Salt Lake City: Bookcraft, 1954–56), 1:32.

2. Hagigah, 1.1, in *The Mishnah,* trans. Herbert Danby (Oxford: Oxford University Press, 1992), 211.

3. Joseph Smith, *Teachings of the Prophet Joseph Smith,* sel. Joseph F. Smith (Salt Lake City: Deseret Book, 1976), 392.

Chapter Thirteen
During the Savior's Mortal Ministry

1. "There Is a Green Hill Far Away," *Hymns of The Church of Jesus Christ of Latter-day Saints* (Salt Lake City: The Church of Jesus Christ of Latter-day Saints, 1985), 194.

2. *The New Greek Interlinear New Testament,* trans. Robert K. Brown and Philip W. Comfort (Wheaton, Ill.: Tyndale House, 1990), 129, translates the Greek word as "family."

3. Bruce R. McConkie, *Doctrinal New Testament Commentary,* 3 vols. (Salt Lake City: Bookcraft, 1965–73), 1:461.

Illustrations

Page i *So They Brought Their Little Children,* by Elspeth Young, courtesy of Al Young Studios. Copyright 2011. All Rights Reserved. For prints, visit www.alyoung.com.

Page x *She Kept All These Things in Her Heart,* by Howard Lyon, © Howard Lyon.

Pages 2–3 Painting by Margaret W. Tarrant, © Medici/Mary Evans

Page 6 *Be It unto Me,* by Liz Lemon Swindle, © Liz Lemon Swindle.

Page 10 *According to Thy Word,* by Elspeth Young, courtesy of Al Young Studios. Copyright 2008. All Rights Reserved. For prints, visit www.alyoung.com.

Page 14 *Behold the Handmaid of the Lord,* by Elspeth Young, courtesy of Al Young Studios. Copyright 2012. All Rights Reserved.

Page 16 *Betrothal of the Holy Virgin and Saint Joseph,* by James Jacques Joseph Tissot. Brooklyn Museum of Art, New York, USA/The Bridgeman Art Library International/Corbis.

Page 20 *Annunciation to Mary,* by Joseph Brickey, © Joseph Brickey.

Page 24 *The Annunciation,* by Carl Heinrich Bloch, © Image Asset Management Ltd./SuperStock.

Page 27 *Study for the Face of the Virgin Mary of the Annunciation*, by Leonardo Da Vinci.

ILLUSTRATIONS

Page 28 — *Annunciation to Joseph,* by Joseph Brickey, © Joseph Brickey.

Page 32 — *Madonna in Prayer,* artist unknown, © Getty Images/SuperStock.

Page 37 — *Madonna and Child,* Sassoferrato (1609–85, Italian), © SuperStock/SuperStock.

Page 40 — *The Visitation,* by Carl Heinrich Bloch, National History Museum, Frederiksborg Castle, Denmark, © SuperStock/SuperStock.

Page 43 — *Refuge,* by Liz Lemon Swindle, © Liz Lemon Swindle.

Page 46 — *Madonna and Child,* by Jourdan Adolphe Jourdan (1825–89, French), Gallery and Museum, Stirling, Scotland, © Bridgeman Art Library, London/SuperStock.

Page 50 — *Journey to Bethlehem,* by Joseph Brickey, © Joseph Brickey.

Pages 54–55 — *No Room in the Inn,* by Joseph Brickey, © Joseph Brickey.

Page 59 — *She Shall Bring Forth a Son,* by Liz Lemon Swindle, © Liz Lemon Swindle.

Page 60 — *Behold the Lamb of God,* by Walter Rane, © Walter Rane.

Page 64 — *A Light unto the World,* © Greg Olsen. By arrangement with Greg Olsen Art Publishing Inc., Meridian, Idaho, 83642. For more information on art prints by Greg Olsen, please contact Greg Olsen Art Publishing Inc. at 1-208-888-2585.

Page 68 — *Flight to Egypt,* William Hole, "Life of Jesus" (c. 1890) plate 9, Mary Evans Picture Library.

Page 71 — *The Wise Men Journeying to Bethlehem,* illustration for "The Life of Christ," c. 1886–94, James Jacques Joseph Tissot (1836–1902), Brooklyn Museum of Art, New York, USA/The Bridgeman Art Library International.

Page 72 — *Child of Grace,* by Liz Lemon Swindle, © Liz Lemon Swindle.

Page 76 — *In Favor with God,* by Simon Dewey, © Simon Dewey.

Page 79 — *When Did He Know,* by Liz Lemon Swindle, © Liz Lemon Swindle.

ILLUSTRATIONS

Pages 80–81 *Jesus in the Temple,* by Carl Heinrich Bloch, National History Museum, Frederiksborg Castle, Denmark, © SuperStock/SuperStock.

Pages 84–85 *The Youth of Our Lord,* 1847–56, Unknown artist, © Getty Images/Photo by John Rogers Herbert/The Bridgeman Art Library.

Page 86 *Mother,* by Liz Lemon Swindle, © Liz Lemon Swindle.

Page 90 *Wedding at Cana,* by Carl Heinrich Bloch, National History Museum, Frederiksborg Castle, Denmark, © SuperStock/SuperStock.

Page 95 *Jesus Preaching by the Seashore,* illustration for "The Life of Christ," c. 1886–96, James Jacques Joseph Tissot (1836–1902). The Bridgeman Art Library International/Corbis.

Page 98 *The Pieta,* by Joseph Brickey, © Joseph Brickey.

Page 103 *Crucifixion,* by Carl Heinrich Bloch, National History Museum, Frederiksborg Castle, Denmark, © SuperStock/SuperStock.

Page 104 *Blessed Is She That Believed,* by Elspeth Young, courtesy of Al Young Studios. Copyright 2008. All Rights Reserved. For prints, visit www.alyoung.com.